INTERTWINED ROOTS

W. A. Hanna

Intertwined Roots

AN ULSTER-SCOT PERSPECTIVE ON
HERITAGE, HISTORY, HOSTILITY AND HOPE
IN NORTHERN IRELAND

the columba press

First published in 2000 by
the columba press
55A Spruce Avenue, Stillorgan Industrial Park,
Blackrock, Co Dublin

Cover by Bill Bolger
The cover picture is *The West Prospect of the Giant's Causeway* by
Suzanna Drury, reproduced with the kind permission of the
National Museums & Galleries of Northern Ireland.
Origination by The Columba Press
Printed in Ireland by Colour Books Ltd, Dublin

ISBN 1 85607 290 8

The Giant's Causeway

The actual 'causeway' part of the Giant's Causeway points out to sea. A
fanciful tale from long ago suggests that it was built by a legendary
giant as a land bridge between Scotland and the north of Ireland – and
indeed there are similar geological structures on the island of Staffa off
the Scottish coast, which may have contributed to the myth. The old
make-believe story may serve as a reminder of the close links between
the two.

Acknowledgements

I wish to thank all those who have given so willingly of their expertise
and time in one way or another to make this book possible – Bill Boyd,
Harry Bunting, Victor Clarke, Bill Dunlop, John Erskine, Adrian Glover,
Harold Gray, Bob Hanna, Finlay Holmes, David Irwin, Thelma King,
Patrick McGarry, Des McFaul, Bill McReynolds, Duncan Morrow,
Trevor Ringland, Roger and Jenny Smyth, John Watts, and Seán O
Boyle and the staff of The Columba Press. In particular, I wish to thank
my wife, Pat, who encouraged me to write it, for her patience and help
throughout the whole project.

Will Hanna

Contents

Preface

The Ulster-Scots of today are the descendants of lowland Scots who began to settle in Ulster in significant numbers in the first decade of the seventeenth century. There has inevitably been intermingling and intermarriage down the years, and they are not such a close-knit or clearly identifiable group as formerly. Nevertheless, those with an Ulster-Scot connection probably still make up the greater number of the majority community in Northern Ireland. This book looks at them against the background of their past history, and in the broader context of changing circumstances at the close of the twentieth century.

For the most part Presbyterians when they first arrived, the Ulster-Scots experienced religious, social and economic discrimination in one form or another, and in varying degree, at the hands of an Anglican Establishment for over two hundred years. Indeed, for much of this time the term 'Protestant' was restricted to adherents of the Church of Ireland. Nonconformists were usually referred to separately as Dissenters – an epithet that in Ulster was almost synonymous with Presbyterians, but also included small numbers of others, such as Baptists and Quakers and, after the mid-eighteenth century, Methodists. It was only as oppressive legislation was gradually withdrawn over the next hundred years or so, that the political and communal interests of Ulster-Scot Presbyterians began to converge and merge with those of fellow-Protestants of Anglican persuasion and of mainly Anglo-Irish stock. Nowadays they are generally all grouped together as Protestants and, regardless of where in these islands their ancestors came from, (or whether they were Protestant refugees from the continent, like the Huguenots from France), most of them consider themselves British.

Some of the attitudes and attributes, both good and bad, of the present-day more inclusive Protestant and broadly unionist community in Northern Ireland probably derive from old Dissenter traits and tendencies, and may be better understood in the light of the history of the major Ulster-Scot and largely Presbyterian component within it. Yet paradoxically, those aware or appreciative of their Ulster-Scot identity not infrequently find it has been subsumed under the wider general grouping, and their position and perspective all too often ignored or disregarded by overseas authors, commentators or politicians, who may be unfamiliar with their background and ignorant of their history.

Hence Part One of this study of the Ulster-Scots, and how they have become an integral part of the majority community in the province, deals mainly with their past. The relationship down the years between the peoples of the north of Ireland and of Scotland provides a backdrop to the story of the seventeenth-century Scottish planters and those who followed them. Outside academic circles or special interest groups, little may be known about the early difficulties they experienced, and these are referred to in an overview of their history. Although much has been written elsewhere about those who emigrated in the eighteenth century to the American colonies – where they became known as the 'Scotch-Irish' – for convenience and completeness a summary of their involvement in the advancement of their new homeland is included as an Appendix to Part One. In Part Two, Protestant/ unionist perceptions about certain aspects of their heritage and culture are noted, and some of the concerns that continue to cause division between the communities are considered. In Part Three the course of the 'peace process' is traced through media reports and headlines that not only highlight the main events, but also reveal the stresses and strains, the hopes and fears of the people of the province, and reflect their mood. A summary of the Good Friday Agreement, and the texts of several interesting and relevant documents are given as Appendices to Parts Two and Three.

Introduction

Six hundred million years ago Scotland and the north of Ireland lay alongside Newfoundland and the North America/Greenland land mass, separated from England and southern Ireland by an ocean known to geologists as the Proto-Atlantic or Iapetus Ocean.[1] They were welded to southern Britain and Ireland as Iapetus closed and the ancestral continents of Europe and North America collided and fused about four hundred million years ago. They remained firmly attached to these offshore islands of Europe when the rifting that initiated the opening up and later widening of the northern part of the present Atlantic Ocean occurred around one hundred million years ago.

More recently, geology students at the Queen's University of Belfast, when choosing a distinctive T-shirt for their student society, briefly and light-heartedly considered using a logo that incorporated the slogan or motto 'Reopen Iapetus'. This would have been, in effect, a coded political statement, readily decipherable by those who know that the geological suture formed by the closure of Iapetus, cuts the east coast of Ireland near the ancient border of an erstwhile large and powerful province of Ulster, whose southern limits once extended as far as the Boyne.[2] Admittedly in Ireland (unlike Britain where the border between England and Scotland roughly follows the Iapetus suture) the lines of the old provincial boundary and the geological suture diverge as they continue inland. Nevertheless, the slogan (never seriously considered because of its potential political sensitivity) illustrates that particular sense of humour that enables the people of the province to laugh with each other and at themselves from time to time despite their political divisions.

There have always been close links between the people of the north of Ireland and of Scotland. According to that ancient collection of stories known as the Ulster cycle, which extols the exploits of the province's mythological heroes of two thousand or so years ago, the sons of Usnach, having incurred the wrath of the king of Ulster, sought refuge in Scotland. Ulster's legendary champion, Cú Chulainn, is said to have perfected his fighting skills there, at the martial arts school of Scáthach, a warrior woman renowned for her prowess and ferocity. She must have taught him well, for *Táin Bó Cuailnge* – described by Thomas Kinsella as 'the centre-piece of the Ulster cycle' and 'the oldest vernacular epic in Western literature' – tells how he later defended the province single-handed against 'the men of Ireland'! They had attacked when, to quote the *Táin* again, 'the men of Ulster' were laid low by a curse – evidenced in times of crisis by the onset of severe pains, extreme weakness and profound lethargy.[3] (The paraphrased translation by Lady Gregory, and the more literal one by Kinsella of the earliest version of the story, are among the most readable available today.)

This specific introductory reference to archaic north-south divisions in Ireland may serve to highlight the fact that although present divisions are rooted in centuries of more recent history, that history has often been distorted by the conflicting myths and perceptions of a divided society. The statue of Cú Chulainn in the General Post Office, Dublin, is a memorial to the republican 'martyrs' of the 1916 Easter Rebellion; a large painting of him on a gable wall in loyalist East Belfast honours him as the 'ancient defender of Ulster'.

PART ONE

The Past

CHAPTER ONE

Old Irish-Scottish Links

The Ancient Peoples

Isobel Henderson, a well-known authority on the Picts, has written, 'If we Scots like to think of ourselves as something distinct from an Irish colony, then it is the spirit of the tribes who went to make up the Picts that we must invoke'.[4]

Towards the close of the third century AD, the Romans began to use the name *Picti*, apparently as a collective name for the Caledones and other tribes north of the Forth-Clyde line. Those early English chroniclers who located another group of Picts in Galloway, are thought by most modern experts to have been mistaken. Celtic authors, when writing in Latin, used *Picti* in the same sense as the Romans had done. In Irish and Scots Gaelic, however, the name *Cruithni* served for both the Picts of Scotland and the ancient pre-Celtic peoples of Ireland – in particular those in the north, where they survived into historical times. *Cruithni* is the Q-Celtic (Goidelic/Gaelic) version of the P-Celtic (Brythonic/Brittonic) name *Pretani*. Our islands were known in antiquity as Albion and Ierne, but following the voyage of Pytheas about 325 BC, were referred to collectively in some classical sources as the Pretanic Islands. *Britannia*, the name the Romans used for their island province, was probably a corruption.

Opinion is divided on whether the Picts of Scotland and the *Cruithni* or Cruthin of Ulster were essentially the same people. Many authorities, noting the more obvious linguistic and cultural differences (such as the Pictish custom of reckoning succession through the female line) argue that they were not. However, Eoin MacNeill (co-founder of the Gaelic League, and one-time

Professor of Early Irish History) firmly believed that both were of the same Pretanic stock.[5] More recently, that eminent churchman and historian, Cardinal Tomás Ó Fiaich, apropos of the coming of the Celts to Ireland, wrote, 'With their arrival a new era had begun in Ireland. The Picts in the north and other pre-Celtic peoples were overthrown.'[6] Moreover, St Colmcille – possibly better or more widely known as Scotland's St Columba – was a contemporary of both Picts and Cruthin and may not have distinguished between them. He evidently thought it expedient, when planning his mission to the Picts, to enlist the help of two Cruthinic monks from Ireland – Comgall, founder and Abbot of the monastery at Bangor, in Co Down, and Cainneach (Canice or Kenneth) later Abbot of Aghaboe.[7] Opinion is also divided on whether the Picts and the Cruthin were basically pre-Celtic or early Celtic people.

Older histories of Galloway and the south-west of Scotland refer to a little-known settlement, apparently mainly of Cruthin from the north of Ireland, in these regions. Unlike the much better-known migration of the Dál Riata to Argyll, there is no tradition or even suggestion that kings, princes or other leaders accompanied them, so it is not surprising that no great importance has been attached to the movement by modern national historians, and many ignore it altogether. This author has noted elsewhere that historians of the nineteenth century wrote of such a migration with considerable certainty and confidence, describing the settlers variously as 'Irish Picts', 'Cruthin or Irish Picts', 'Galloway Cruthin' or 'Galloway Picts'.[8] According to George Chalmers the main Cruthinic migration to Galloway occurred in the eighth century AD and was followed by 'fresh swarms from the Irish hive in the ninth and tenth centuries'.[9] Local historian Peter McKerlie considered that the movement began in the sixth century and continued 'until the Ulster settlers were so numerous as to become the dominant people'.[10] They both argued that the name Pict was introduced to Galloway with the Cruthin and referred to Ulster immigrants rather than to indigenous groups. If some such movement to Galloway did indeed occur, and if

appreciable numbers of Cruthin did settle in this part of
Scotland, then bearing in mind the inclusive use of the Gaelic
name *Cruithni*, any confusion over the location of Picts there by
the early chroniclers may be readily understood.

Two relatively recent, authoritative and scholarly works by
Professors C. Thomas[11] and W. F. H. Nicolaisen[12] (both of whom
cite the evidence of archaeology and of placenames, especially
around the Rhinns of Galloway), lend support to these old theories of a significant movement of people from north-east Ireland
to south-west Scotland – though probably at the earlier date and
possibly not in the numbers suggested above. Their migration
was apparently simultaneous with, if separate from, the better-
attested movement of the Dál Riata to Argyll and the west of
Scotland. Professor Nicolaisen is careful to point out that place-
names alone cannot confirm a possible Cruthinic connection.
However, the old view that these settlers may have been pre-
dominately Cruthin is enhanced by the suggestion of John
McQueen that 'Kreenie' (a local name once applied to poor folk
of the Rhinns, but no longer in use today) derives from the original Gaelic name *Cruithni*.[13]

Ireland and the Scots of Dalriada

Groups of the north Ulster tribe, the Dál Riata, had probably
been settling in western Scotland for a number of years before
Fergus Mór and his brothers, the sons of Erc of the royal house
of the tribe, followed them. They left their ancestral capital of
Dunseverick (a few miles from the Giant's Causeway), established themselves in Argyll, and founded the Scottish kingdom
of Dalriada. It is generally accepted that this occurred in or
around AD 500. Though perhaps not the first king of his fledg-
ling nation, nor the forefather of all the early kings of Dalriada,
and despite possible deficiencies in the genealogical and regnal
records, Fergus Mór is regarded by many as the progenitor of
the royal line of the Scots – and hence a distant ancestor of the
present queen of the United Kingdom of Great Britain and
Northern Ireland.[14] It was only after a long period of fluctuating

fortunes, however, that the descendants of these sixth century *Scotti* – as raiders from Ireland had been called from Roman times – supplanted the Picts as the dominant power in the land, and eventually gave their name to Scotland. From time to time both the indigenous Picts and the settler Scots suffered grievously from repeated Viking attacks on their territory. It has been suggested that shortly before Kenneth MacAlpin, king of Dalriada and possibly a claimant to the Pictish throne through their matrilineal system of succession, finally defeated them about 843, the Picts had sustained a particularly severe setback at the hands of a Viking army.[15] There are also dark stories of a slaughter of Pictish leaders invited to a Scots banquet about that time. Whatever the reason, the Picts virtually disappear from history after that date.

Most authorities agree that the Dál Riata were one of the Érainn group of loosely related Celtic tribes. Ulster derives its name from the most powerful of the Érainn tribes in the north, the ancient Ulaid, whose much diminished descendants survived well into the middle ages as the Dál Fiatach.[16] T. F. O'Rahilly, reasoning from age-old origin legends as well as linguistic evidence, deduced that, after the Cruthin, the Érainn were one of the earliest groups to settle in Ireland; that they and the Laginian tribes that arrived later, were non-Goidelic Celts, who originally would have spoken a P-Celtic language; and that only the latest Celtic invaders, the Goidels, were Q-Celts.[17] Be that as it may, there is no doubt that by the time of their migration to Argyll the Dál Riata, in common with all the other tribes of Ireland regardless of origin or date of arrival, spoke a Q-Celtic language, and it was they who introduced Gaelic to Scotland. O'Rahilly's views, once highly regarded in certain circles, are at variance with current received opinion,[18] and cannot be confirmed or disproved. The same, of course, applies to all other theories about this period, whether based on popular mythology or scholarly speculation. At all events, a number of eminent authorities today, irrespective of what they may think of O'Rahilly's conclusions, seem to share some of his scepticism about the historicity of the (often politically motivated) regnal records and royal pedigrees produced by early Irish 'synthetic historians' and genealogists.[19]

Ethnicity, determined as much by cultural influences as by genetic ancestry, can change over time, as individuals or whole groups become (or are accepted as) part of another group. Such a change may eventually lead to an erroneous perception of genetic origins. This, some would suggest, may have happened to the Dál Riata *Scotti* long before they ever left Ireland! Although, as John Bannerman has commented, 'it is arguable that the advent of Fergus Mór is the single most important event in Scotland's history',[20] the origins of the Dalriada Scots remain shrouded in the mists and myths of pre-historic Ireland.

The Welsh Britons called the Irish *Gwyddyl*, which name the Irish seem to have adopted for themselves as *Goídil*.[21] Early Irish historians and genealogists closely linked the ancestry of the Goidels or Gaels to descent from a remote ancestor Míl, whose two sons, Éber and Éremón, allegedly led the last Celtic invasion of Ireland, conquered the island, and divided it between them.[22] In his authoritative book, *Irish Kings and High-Kings*, Francis Byrne, Professor of Early Irish History at University College, Dublin, has noted that according to the earliest edition of the *Lebor Gabála* (Book of Invasions) only the Eóganachta and the Connachta (including their dominant Uí Néill branch) were descended from them. It would appear that 'parity of esteem' (to use the current catchphrase) was not accorded to other tribal groups, some of whom were regarded as *aithech-tuatha* – that is inferior or 'unfree tribes'. Later, according to Professor Byrne, 'other dynasties of local importance were provided by the synthetic historians with a line of descent from other sons of Míl, whose family underwent an alarming, if posthumous, increase. Even the more prominent of the Cruthin and the Érainn were brought into the Milesian scheme.'[23]

However, despite having been admitted into the 'Milesian' extended family, and credited with the most prestigious ancestry, the Cruthin and the Érainn tribes in Ulster continued to suffer from the aggressive expansion of the powerful Cenél nEógain branch of the northern Uí Néill. Almost certainly it was some such pressure that, notwithstanding their acquired pedigree, prompted the royal house of the Dál Riata to move over to Scotland, and also contributed to the later loss of their Irish lands.[24]

Undoubtedly many with impeccable Gaelic lineage and status followed them to west Scotland. Probably the most famous was Colmcille, who was a prince of the Cenél Conaill branch of the northern Uí Néill, and related to the high-king of Ireland. He also had family connections with the royal house of the Dalriada Scots through his paternal grandmother Erca, who was a daughter of Loarn Mór – one of the sons of Erc who had made the historic move to Scotland. Loarn was possibly the first king of Dalriada – or perhaps 'joint king' for a time with his younger brother, Fergus.[25] Besides founding the famous monastery on Iona and taking the gospel to the Picts, Colmcille consecrated Aedán (great-grandson of Fergus Mór) as king, accompanied him to the important Convention of Druim Cett in Ireland, and did much to enhance his prestige and that of his emergent Scots kingdom.

Later, after they gained control of the Pictish territories during the ninth century, the Scots kings began to look south. By the early twelfth century the Borders, Lothian, Strathclyde and Galloway (with their mix of pre-Celtic, Brythonic and Goidelic Celtic, not to mention Angle, Norse and Norman influences, both genetic and cultural) had become Scotticised, and had been brought under the Scottish crown in the process.[26]

Comings and Goings

Brief mention has been made above of both the Vikings and the Normans. In Ireland, although they founded the first towns, the Vikings (whether Norsemen or Danes) seldom controlled large areas of the country as they did in northern and eastern England, as well as in the northern and western isles and in parts of the mainland of Scotland. The Normans had been in

England a little short of a century when Dermot MacMurrough
arrived to seek their help in recovering his kingdom of Leinster,
from which he had been driven as the result of bitter feuding
with other Irish kings. The arrival in Ireland in 1169 of a contin-
gent of thirty knights, with their men-at-arms and archers, in response to his appeal and invitation, marked the start of the so-
called 'Anglo-Norman invasion' – though many of the leaders,
including the FitzGeralds, had closer birth and blood connections with Wales than with England, and most of their bowmen
were Flemish or Welsh.

In spite of initial military superiority, the Norman conquest
of Ireland was never complete. Indeed, much lost territory was
regained by Irish chiefs, especially after they began to bring in
heavily armed Norse-Scottish mercenaries in the second half of
the thirteenth century.[27] These 'gallowglasses', as they were
called, were often rewarded with grants of land. Others from
Scotland, such as the great Lord of Galloway, the Earls of
Carrick and of Atholl, and even the more humble Bysets, had
earlier received lands in Ulster[28] – in this case from the Normans
for services rendered to them. Another facet of the Norman
story is that many of their leading families intermarried with
ruling Gaelic ones. Their gradual assimilation into Irish society
developed over the ensuing years as some of their offspring,
who were often fostered with Irish chiefs, adopted Gaelic culture
and customs and became 'more Irish than the Irish themselves'.[29]

Robert de Brus was one of several Norman nobles given
lands in Scotland during the second quarter of the twelfth century,
by the francophile king, David I. In 1306 a descendant of both,
Robert the Bruce, son-in-law of the Earl of Ulster, was crowned
King of Scots. Having stabbed a rival claimant to the throne in
church, he incurred excommunication and inevitably lost the
support of many Scots nobles. Within months he was heavily
defeated by the English and had to flee, seeking temporary
refuge for periods in the north-west, in various Scottish islands
and possibly in Rathlin off the north coast of Ulster – where

some say he met his legendary 'try, try, try again' spider! Over the next five years, however, Robert gradually gained support throughout Scotland, and eventually subdued any remaining pockets of disaffection or opposition. He then began to drive the English out of towns they had occupied and garrisoned in the south and east of the country. At Bannockburn in 1314, he won a resounding victory over the large and impressive army that had marched north to relieve Stirling, the only English stronghold left in Scotland.

The next year Robert sent an army to Ireland under the command of his brother Edward, possibly to follow up that victory and divert English pressure from his own borders by attacking their Irish colony. Edward, who was welcomed and supported by Donal O'Neill and a number of Gaelic chiefs, was crowned king of Ireland in May, 1316. By September, when Robert himself joined the expedition for a period, Edward had established control over most of Ulster. Together the brothers were dominant in the field and virtually unopposed as they marched on Dublin early the next year. However, lacking a siege train, they were unable to take the strongly defended city and retired to the north. Thereafter their enterprise lost much of its momentum; Robert returned to Scotland, and Edward was killed in battle in 1318.[30] Although ultimately defeated, the Bruce invasion of Ireland further weakened English authority, which was already being undermined by the resurgence of some Gaelic chiefs and the disaffection of a number of prominent Anglo-Normans.

The cumulative result, despite sporadic efforts to reverse the situation, was that effective English control started to decline about this time. Furthermore, a significant Gaelic recovery began to take shape around the beginning of the fifteenth century – though this was at a local rather than a co-ordinated national level. A number of Irish chieftains recovered a considerable amount of lost land, and some of the aristocratic Anglo-Irish families (such as the Desmond branch of the FitzGeralds) became increasingly Gaelicised.[31] However, by the end of the century, in the final phase of the long dispute between the houses of

Lancaster and York, Henry Tudor – 'the nearest thing to royalty the Lancastrian party possessed' – had seized the throne of England and been crowned as Henry VII. He had also disposed of two young pretenders, whose claims had been recognised by Yorkist supporters in Ireland, including the great FitzGerald Earls of Kildare and of Desmond.[32] Thereafter, during the sixteenth century his Tudor successors, concerned that powerful rival nations such as France and Spain might likewise attempt to use Ireland as a base for operations against England, generally adopted a more assertive and aggressive policy towards their Irish colony.[33]

Meanwhile, in Co Antrim, Margery, the last Byset heiress, had married John Mór of Isla and Cantire (brother of Donal of Harlaw, Lord of the Isles) in 1399,[34] so when, nearly a century later, the Lordship of the Isles was forfeited, many islanders began to move to former Byset, now MacDonnell lands in the Glens of Antrim. While some settled there, others as 'redshank' mercenaries crossed intermittently when required. Those who followed them down the years to this north-east corner of Ulster – even after the Reformation spread to Scotland – were, like their chiefs, mainly Roman Catholics. This trend was temporarily interrupted early in the seventeenth century, when their chief, Sir Randal MacDonnell, later created 1st Earl of Antrim, invited lowland Scots into the Route district.[35] Such a one-off move undoubtedly pleased the newly-crowned Protestant Scots king of England, who had recently confirmed Sir Randal in his Irish estates, despite his Catholic background and the fact that he had fought on the rebel side at Kinsale. Most Scots who emigrated to other parts of Ulster at that time and throughout the century were mainly lowlanders and generally Presbyterians.

CHAPTER TWO

The Ulster-Scots

The Plantation of Ulster and the 1641 Rebellion
While English authority had been declining, the O'Neills, descendants of one of the major dynasties or septs of the Cenél nEógain branch of the northern Uí Néill, had been regaining ground west of the Bann and in Tyrone. By 1450 their Clandeboye offshoot had spread east to the coast of south Antrim and north Down. However, the O'Donnells, descendants of the Cenél Conaill, the other main branch of the northern Uí Néill, controlled Tyrconnell.[36] In the 1560s Shane O'Neill (known as the Proud) sought to confirm his supremacy in Ulster by attacking both the O'Donnells in the north-west and the Scottish MacDonnells in the north-east.[37] Initially victorious over both, he eventually was defeated by the O'Donnells, and having metaphorically lost the head when he inexplicably sought shelter with the MacDonnells, did in fact lose it after being murdered by them.[38]

Despite such fratricidal feuds, the most united, determined and sustained resistance to the sixteenth century Tudor conquest of Ireland occurred in Ulster towards the end of Elizabeth I's reign. Hugh O'Neill, though holding the English title Earl of Tyrone, was recognised by his people as the chief of his clan – The O'Neill. He was also a nephew of Shane, but more subtle and shrewd than his uncle. Instead of feuding, he formed an alliance with Red Hugh, the chief of the O'Donnells, and other northern leaders, and together they posed a formidable threat to the English. Initially their rebel army won a series of significant victories in the north.[39] In late 1601 they marched south to join a Spanish army that had arrived to support them, but was now besieged at Kinsale by the English. There they suffered their first major (and in the event, decisive) defeat on Christmas Eve that year – a battle that has been described elsewhere as Ireland's Culloden.[40] O'Donnell fled to Spain, while O'Neill had no option but to withdraw to the north. Two years later he made his submission to the Lord Deputy, unaware that Elizabeth, the last of the Tudors, had died a week earlier. He was the last of the defeated rebel leaders to submit and had to renounce that most prestigious of Irish titles – The O'Neill. However, his earldom of Tyrone was restored to him by the new Stewart king of England. At the same time Rory, the new chief of the O'Donnells, was made Earl of Tyrconnell.[41] Although they were able to retain most of their lands, nonetheless O'Neill and O'Donnell felt themselves increasingly harassed by the new officers of the Crown.

Meanwhile, before the war had ended, Conn O'Neill of Clandeboye had been imprisoned on a charge of 'treason'. His escape to Scotland, and subsequent pardon, were arranged by two shrewd Scotsmen, Hugh Montgomery and James Hamilton, as part of a bargain by which they each received a third share of Conn's extensive estates in north Down.[42] Some would say they conned poor Conn! Prior to the accession of the Scots king, James VI, to the throne of England as James I, Scottish settlers had not been welcomed in Ireland by the English authorities.[43] Now, however, Hamilton and Montgomery were able to invite many fellow countrymen into their newly acquired estates, which they further enlarged by astute purchases in south Antrim and north Down. These private enterprise settlements provided an example and bridgehead for the subsequent official 'plantation' of most of the other counties of Ulster. Plans for this were set in motion in 1607 after the 'Flight of the Earls' of Tyrone and Tyrconnell, whose sudden and secret departure was regarded as treasonable. Their lands were confiscated and, by the 'Articles of Plantation' issued in 1609, made available to 'English or inland (i.e. lowland) Scots' for settlement.[44]

There had been earlier, less successful attempts at plantation in other parts of Ireland by both the Tudor queens of England – the Roman Catholic Mary as well as the Protestant Elizabeth.[45] The greater number of those who settled and stayed in Ulster in the seventeenth century were from Scotland, and the settlement soon acquired a distinctively Scottish character especially in the eastern counties.[46] A majority of these Scots came from the south-west of the country, the region to which many Cruthin had migrated earlier, and it is not unreasonable to suppose that a significant number may have been descendants of Ulster emigrants of an earlier age. Some may possibly have recalled old folk-memories of dim distant Irish origins.[47] Indeed 'The Plantation of Ulster' has even been described as 'The Great Return'. However, most of those who came almost certainly did not do so as Irishmen of any ilk. They came rather as hard-headed lowland Scots, and because of the course the Reformation had taken in Scotland, most were Presbyterian.

James's son and successor, Charles I, antagonised his people, not only in England but also in Scotland and Ireland, by his high-handed policies in church and state. His self-inflicted troubles in Scotland arose over his attempts to bring the Scottish church into closer conformity with the Church of England, which provoked the Scottish National Covenant of 1638. At the same time his Lord Deputy, Thomas Wentworth, was trying to enforce similar policies in Ireland, where Presbyterian Scots ministers and settlers were compelled to conform and renounce the Scottish Covenant by taking the so-called 'Black Oath'. Even the established Church of Ireland (though Anglican) was not immune, its Irish Articles (which were essentially Calvinist in content) being replaced by the Thirty-Nine Articles of the Church of England.[48]

During this period of instability, resentment at their lot had been growing among the indigenous Irish. In 1641 a sudden and savage onslaught on Protestant settlements across Ulster signalled the onset of open rebellion. One of the leaders, Sir Phelim O'Neill, claimed he was acting in support of the king and produced a forged document in evidence of this.[49] Initially the in-

surgents indicated that all Scots would be spared. The reasons
for this are unclear – perhaps because of a perceived Gaelic link,
or in the hope that the Scots, with their grievances, might also
rebel, or at least remain aloof. Whatever the reason, such leniency
did not last long.[50] Although many of the accounts of the ensuing massacres were undoubtedly exaggerated, they contributed,
nevertheless, to the scarcely less brutal reaction first of a Scots
army dispatched to deal with the situation, and later of the puni-
tive campaign of Cromwell. That atrocities against the settlers
did in fact occur would seem to be irrefutable, but perhaps the
most enduring result of the events associated with the 1641 rebellion was that they became ingrained in the folk-memory of
the Protestant community and have provided a ready rallying
call in times of crisis and danger ever since.[51]

In 1642, alarmed by reports of these massacres, the Scots
Parliament sent an army under Major-General Monro to protect
the planters and settlers in Ulster. It was Monro's army chaplains and officer-elders who formed the first Presbytery in
Ireland.[52] The Civil War also started in England that year, and
further complicated the issue in Ireland, where several armies
were in the field at the time. Here it was known as 'The War of
the Three Kingdoms', and loyalties towards the king or the parliamentary party shifted during its course.[53] Both had supporters in Ireland, but concentrated their main effort on first winning the war in England. Meanwhile Old English and Irish
fought side by side in a Confederate Catholic Army; but the former wanted little more than religious concessions, while the latter hoped in addition to regain lost lands. Owen Roe O'Neill,
nephew of Hugh O'Neill, led a Catholic Army of Ulster to a
major victory over Monro's Scots at Benburb in 1645, but failed
to follow it up.

When the parliamentarians finally won the war in England,
and Charles I was tried and executed in 1649, the Ulster Presbytery condemned their actions,[54] which did not endear them to
Parliament or to Oliver Cromwell. He came later that year with
yet another army to impose the authority of the new régime

throughout Ireland. This he effected efficiently if ruthlessly, as at the storming of Drogheda and of Wexford, since when his name has been anathematised in Irish folk-memory. Nevertheless, around 30,000 disbanded rebel troops were later allowed to leave for France or Spain. However, it was decreed in an Act of Settlement involving a drastic redistribution of land, that those Irish landowners who had taken part in the rebellion would lose their lands, while those who had not would be 'transplanted' to Connacht and Clare, and compensated with land there.[55] Moreover, troublesome Ulster-Scots were also to be moved to the south-west, well away from support in Scotland; a 'black-list' (which included a Hanna!) was drawn up, but this particular plan was allowed to lapse.[56]

Close links between Scotland and the Ulster-Scots continued, however. In an age when considerable emphasis was placed on religious faith and belief, the Church of Scotland supported the infant Presbyterian Church in Ireland from time to time by sending over ministers on a temporary basis. Following 'The Restoration' and the return of Charles II in 1660, Presbyterians (and other Dissenters) continued to suffer religious, civil and economic disabilities under a restored Anglican Establishment. Later there was some relaxation of policy in Ireland towards Nonconformists and Roman Catholics, and in 1672 Charles granted a *regium donum* to Presbyterian ministers.[57] In Scotland, opposition to an imposed episcopal system was particularly strong in the south-west. Here persecution reached a climax in the 'killing times' in Galloway, forcing many Covenanters to seek refuge in Ulster.[58]

The Williamite War and the Anglican Ascendancy

James II, a zealous Roman Catholic, succeeded his brother in 1685. He soon began to promote the interests of his church in Britain, dismissing Protestants in high office who opposed him and replacing them with Catholics. He enlarged his standing army by enlisting more Roman Catholic officers and recruits, and prorogued Parliament when it requested that Acts of

Parliament should not be set aside by Royal Prerogative. Disquiet and discontent became widespread, and within two years an active revolutionary conspiracy was afoot in England.[59] Meanwhile in Ireland his loyal follower Richard Talbot, created Earl of Tyrconnell in 1685 and appointed Lord Deputy in 1687, had embarked on a similar policy of replacing Protestant judges and army officers with Roman Catholics, with the inevitable result that here too Protestant fears increased.[60]

In November 1688, William, Prince of Orange, James's nephew and son-in-law, having been invited by the conspirators to intervene, landed in Devon. James's subsequent flight to France in November was followed four months later by the joint accession to the throne of his son-in-law and daughter, William and Mary. This 'Bloodless' or 'Glorious Revolution' was not as bloodless in Ireland as it had been in Britain.[61] One of William's major considerations, in accepting the offer of the crown, was to secure the help of a powerful neighbour and save the Dutch Republic from invasion by Louis XIV of France.[62] So when James chose to use Ireland as a base from which he might regain his lost kingdoms, the island became for a time the battlefield of an on-going European war.[63]

The siege of Derry has long been a symbol for the Protestants of Ulster of the resolve and defiance of their forefathers. On 10 December 1688, thirteen apprentice boys shut the gates of the city in the face of Lord Antrim's Catholic redshank regiment that had been sent to replace the Protestant garrison. The siege proper began on 21 April 1689, after James himself, having joined his army some days earlier, decided to approach the walls to offer terms, and was greeted with shouts of 'No Surrender'. By the time it ended 105 days later, with the breaking by relief ships of the boom across the River Foyle, possibly 15,000 troops and civilians had died in battle or bombardment, or from disease and starvation.[64] The first contingents of the Williamite army, commanded by the Duke of Schomberg, landed in Ulster in August 1689, and William himself arrived with reinforcements in June 1690. His army contained not only his own

Dutch regiments, but also Germans, Danes and French refugee Huguenots. His victory at the battle of the Boyne on 12 July 1690, ended any realistic hope James might have had of regaining the throne, and was welcomed in several European states.[65]

Despite the undutiful flight of the king they had fought for, and the untimely departure of their French allies, the Catholic Irish resolutely defended Limerick, and held the line of the Shannon in the west for another year. It was only after 'Aughrim's dread disaster' that their hero of Limerick – the popular and dashing Irish general, Patrick Sarsfield – finally sued for peace. Godert de Ginkel, the Dutch commander of the Williamite army, anxious to get the bulk of his troops back to the continent to defend Holland, signed the treaty of Limerick on behalf of the king in October 1691. Those who would not give allegiance to William and Mary were offered transport to France, and 14,000 men left Ireland. It was agreed that those who stayed would retain their property and the right to practise their profession, and that Catholics in general would regain the rights they had enjoyed under Charles II. However, the Protestant landed gentry in the Irish Parliament in Dublin baulked at such Dutch generosity and refused to ratify the treaty.[66]

In the decade or so after James's defeat more Scots, many of them discouraged by a series of poor harvests at home, moved to Ulster.[67] That the so-called 'Protestant Ascendancy' was in reality an Anglican Ascendancy,[68] is reflected in the legislation of the early eighteenth century. Any concessions that had been made to Dissenters by the Calvinist king, William III, were later withdrawn by his High Church successor, Queen Anne. The Test Act of 1704, which excluded Presbyterians from public office and commissions in the army on the basis of a sacramental test, remained in force until 1780.[69] Moreover the ordination of Presbyterian ministers (unlike that of Roman Catholic priests) was not officially recognised.[70] The validity of the marriages they performed, and the legitimacy of the children of such unions and their right to inherit, could also be challenged. (It was to avoid this possibility that, although few Presbyterians were landowners, some of the better off joined the Church of Ireland.) Admittedly less harsh in other respects than the Penal Laws enacted against Roman Catholics, such discriminatory orders were bitterly resented by Ulster-Scots. These and other grievances (for example rack-renting and the resultant loss of land leases) prompted many thousands to emigrate to the American colonies, particularly between 1717 and 1775.[71] There they were known as the Scotch-Irish, whose legacy to the United States of America is a long list of patriots, pioneers and presidents. (See Appendix to Part One.)

The United Irishmen
Events both in America and in France during the last quarter of the eighteenth century significantly influenced the thinking of many Ulster-Scots. They followed with interest the build-up to, and the course of, the War of Independence in America, in which family and friends were possibly involved. They were also impressed by the idealism evident in the early stages of the French Revolution. So it is hardly surprising that a number of radically minded Presbyterians were responsible for inviting Theobold Wolfe Tone to Belfast, and were associated with him in the founding there in 1791 of the Society of United Irishmen. Their aim was to achieve major parliamentary reform and an end to English control in Ireland by uniting Irishmen of all creeds. Other branches were formed later in Dublin and elsewhere.[72] (Tone was a Church of Ireland barrister from Dublin, but more interested in politics than law. His pamphlet *Argument on Behalf of the Catholics of Ireland* had impressed northern reformers. Today he is regarded and honoured as the founder of Irish republicanism.)

At the same time, sectarian strife flared up intermittently. In 1795, after a skirmish between rival gangs of Protestant Peep o' Day Boys and Catholic Defenders, at The Diamond in Co Armagh, the Orange Order was founded – pledged to defend 'the King and his heirs so long as he or they support the Protestant Ascendancy'.[73] The Orangemen's early activities, however, did not significantly deter recruitment to the United Irishmen. (Some regard the Orange Order as having played, and continuing to play, a vital and honourable role in maintaining their heritage. Today, its most visible function – its commemorative marches – may evoke very different responses in the two main communities in the province.)

In 1797 the government, in the context of war with revolutionary France and aware of impending insurrection by United Irishmen possibly with French help, embarked on a ruthless, pre-emptive campaign to disarm Ulster – an exercise enhanced by effective intelligence.[74] This also led to the arrest of most of the Leinster leaders shortly before the rising was due to start in 1798. It began nonetheless in the south in Co Wexford, where the insurgents had initial successes and established a local republic before being defeated at New Ross and Vinegar Hill. There were horrific atrocities on both sides, but reports of rebel murders at Scullabogue and Wexford Bridge did much to damage the United Irish cause among northern Presbyterians.

The action in Ulster (disarmed the previous year) was badly co-ordinated, and limited to uprisings in the eastern counties of Antrim and Down, which were quickly quelled.[75] While Presbyterians predominated on the rebel side, government troops included the largely Protestant yeomanry (for which the Orange Order was a rich recruiting ground) as well as Irish militia regiments such as the Monaghan Militia, which were mainly Catholic. In the aftermath, one ordained Presbyterian minister and two licentiates were hanged, and others were imprisoned or had to emigrate. The sufferings of the rebellion and the 'killing times' which followed, as well as rumours and reports of alleged failures of northern Catholics to support the call to arms, and of anti-Protestant pogroms in the south, contributed to subsequent disillusionment among former sympathisers and supporters in the north-east – the cradle of so much of the idealism of the United Irishmen.[76]

Causes and Concerns of the Nineteenth Century

The British Government's response to the rebellion was the Union of the Parliaments of Great Britain and of Ireland, which came into effect on 1 January 1801. Though of major importance in the course of Irish history, many nineteenth century events are outwith the scope of this overview. These include Daniel O'Connell's successful agitation for Catholic emancipation, the 'Great Famine' of 1846-49 in which about one million people died, emigration which increased dramatically during the famine years (and continued at a high level throughout the century), and the growth of nationalism and republicanism at home and in emigrant communities abroad.

On a more mundane level, many Ulster-Scot families were involved with the problems of higher education and land tenure. Prior to 1845 Trinity College, Dublin, was the only university in Ireland. Its ethos at that time was Anglican and scholarships were reserved for members of the established Church of Ireland, so Ulster-Scots (especially those wishing to study divinity or medicine) tended to look more to Scotland for a university education. Following the establishment of undenominational Queen's Colleges in Belfast, Cork and Galway in that year, Presbyterian students were able to take advantage of these new higher education facilities. Roman Catholic students, however, were discouraged from attending by their bishops who were unhappy about the lack of church-based facilities for them.[77]

The formation of an Ulster Tenant Right Association and later an Irish Tenant League resulted in a degree of co-operation between Protestants and Roman Catholics in the early 1850s. The Land Act of 1881, based on the principle of 'the three Fs' (fair rents, fixity of tenure and the freedom of the tenant to sell his right of occupancy) was the outcome of agitation organised by the Land League. Presbyterian tenant farmers in Ulster had supported the League's official land reform programme and welcomed the Act, but were dismayed that news of its passage provoked outbreaks of violence in other parts of Ireland, where more radical activists in the League had been pursuing a double agenda.[78] A coincidental by-product of the Act was a further improvement in relations within the Protestant community, as a major cause of resentment against the largely Anglican landlord class was removed. Most of those grievances more specifically attributable to religious discrimination had already been removed by the disestablishment of the Church of Ireland in 1869.[79] The political interests of Protestants as a whole, whether from a Presbyterian or Church of Ireland background, or of Ulster-Scot or Anglo-Irish stock, had begun to merge even earlier.

This trend accelerated as demands for Home Rule increased, and the hierarchy of the Roman Catholic Church, which had supported the Land League, finally came to back the essentially political National League. By this time most Protestants were broadly unionist in outlook. However, the views of Charles Stewart Parnell, a young Protestant landowner from Co Wicklow, differed significantly from those of most of his co-religionists. Although not the founder of either the Land League or the Home Rule League, he was not only president of the former, but also undisputed leader of the Irish Parliamentary Party by the early 1880s. After the passage of the 1881 Land Act, he concentrated his efforts on winning Home Rule for Ireland. In the 1885 General Election his party won most of the Irish seats and held the balance of power in the House of Commons. W. E. Gladstone, leader of the Liberal Party, having chosen to champion Home Rule, became Prime Minister again, but his Home Rule Bills were defeated – the first in 1886 by Liberal defections in the Commons, and the second in 1893 when blocked by the Lords. In 1890, however, Parnell's position as leader of the main Irish party had been called into question following the divorce case in which he was cited as co-respondent. Gladstone had reacted to public opinion and the threat of trouble in the Liberal Party, by calling on Parnell to resign (temporarily at least) as leader of the Irish Parliamentary Party. Parnell's stubborn refusal to comply compounded the divisions in his own party.[80]

Partition

The Irish Parliamentary Party remained deeply divided and ineffective for several years. By 1900 it had been reunited, but not until 1910 did it again hold the balance of power in the Commons. The next year a Parliament Bill was passed and the right of the Lords to reject Bills passed in the Commons was thereby restricted. So when the third Home Rule Bill was introduced in 1912, the Lords were no longer in a position to delay it indefinitely. By now most northern Protestants were strongly opposed to Home Rule, and a massive campaign of resistance to the Bill began. On 28 September 1912, Ulster's 'Solemn League and Covenant' was signed, with well over 470,000 men and women (who signed their own separate declaration) pledging themselves to use 'all means which may be found necessary' to defeat it. An Ulster Volunteer Force was founded in 1913, and a shipment of arms was brought into the province the next year.[81] Similar armed bodies – the Citizen Army and the Irish Volunteers – were established on the nationalist side.

The new Home Rule Bill was passed for the third time in the Commons in 1914, and as the Lords could delay it no longer, became law later the same year – though its implementation was postponed as World War I had begun by then. The Irish Parliamentary Party leadership, used for so long to working constitutionally for Home Rule, agreed to this course of action. The mood in much of the country changed, however, following the Easter Rising and the subsequent executions in 1916. By the end of the war the original terms of the Bill had become almost irrelevant. Apart from the emergence of the Irish Republican Army (IRA) around this time, the details of both the Anglo-Irish War and the Civil War are not pertinent to this short survey.[82] Although a unionist majority ensured that Northern Ireland (comprising six of the nine counties of the province of Ulster) remained within the United Kingdom, an independent twenty-six county Irish Free State emerged. This new nation (which in 1948 became the Republic of Ireland) perceived its roots as Gaelic in culture and Roman Catholic in religion. The tendency persists in certain quarters to define true Irishness in such exclusive terms.

The histories of the two parts of Ireland have been fully documented and discussed in a number of relatively recent publications. The early years after 'partition' were formative ones and determined the course of the relationship between the peoples of the two main traditions in the island for over fifty years. The astute assessments of two distinguished Irish historians regarding this period are not only pertinent but worth quoting at this point.

Professor R. F. Foster, in *Modern Ireland 1600-1972*, observed that 'what matters most about the atmosphere and mentality of twenty-six county Ireland in the 1920s is that the dominant preoccupation of the regime was self-definition against Britain – cultural and political'. He not only noted that 'the regime necessarily laid heavy emphasis on the "Gaelic" nature of the new state', but also described the close relationship between church and state in equally forthright terms. 'From its origins, the Free State government had carefully lined up the Roman Catholic hierarchy on its side, consulting bishops on constitutional matters, and receiving in return powerful support ... In turn, the church made its line clear on social policy ... In education, as in social law, the state followed the Catholic line ...'[83]

Professor J. C. Beckett, in his book *The Anglo-Irish Tradition*, also referred to the same period, and made some very valid and perceptive points about doctrinaire politics in both the North and the South, and about the establishment of a Gaelic and Catholic state in the South. He argued that, 'The Anglo-Irish, had they retained any effective political influence, might at this stage have done something to save Ireland from itself.' They had 'spontaneously announced their readiness to abandon old affiliations and to play their part in making a new Ireland. If they had been allowed to do so in any decisive way they might, perhaps, have convinced the rulers of the Free State that the choice before them was one between fostering the unity of Ireland and confirming its division; ... that to demand territorial unity while emphasising cultural divisions is an irresponsibly dangerous policy. But ... the politicians went their own way; and the new

régime in the South was as markedly Roman Catholic and
Gaelicising as that in the North was Protestant.'

Professor Beckett went on to reflect that the Anglo-Irish in
the South 'might have supplied a link between the opposing
forces, North and South ... the sight of a strong, stable, confident
and influential minority in the Free State would have gone far to
allay the suspicious fears of the Protestants of Ulster. The actual
picture was very different; and to many people it provided
ample proof that those fears had been justified; that Home Rule
did indeed mean Rome Rule; and that the system of government
under which Protestantism was dying in the South would, if allowed to do so, produce the same effect in the North'.[84]

This is very much how northern unionists of the time,
whether of Ulster-Scot or of Anglo-Irish stock, saw the situation.
The early exclusive attitude and approach of both church and
state in the South, evinced in statements of the hierarchy and evidenced in the policies of the party (or parties) in power, were
perceived as a threat to them, and confirmed for them the cor-
rectness of their own equally exclusive policies. In the early
1920s the General Assembly of the Presbyterian Church in
Ireland encouraged those members who remained in the South
'to co-operate wholeheartedly with their Roman Catholic fellow
countrymen in the best interests of their beloved land'.
Unfortunately this approach was not always reciprocated. In
1931, the head of the Roman Catholic Church in Ireland,
Cardinal MacRory is quoted as asserting that 'the Protestant
Church in Ireland' was 'not even a part of the Church of Christ'.
The written submission, of the (Catholic) Irish Episcopal Conference to the New Ireland Forum in 1984, acknowledged the
fact that 'widespread refusal to co-operate with the institutions
of the new state was a marked feature of Catholic attitudes from
the beginning'.[85] Mary Harris, in her book *The Catholic Church
and the Foundation of the Northern Irish State*, suggests that
'Partition had provided a protective cocoon for southern Catholics.
By relieving the Free State of a large Protestant minority, it
allowed the development of a political system exceptionally

well in tune with Catholic thought.' She not only tells how, but explains why, some members of the Roman Catholic hierarchy and clergy actively discouraged their people from playing a positive part in, or giving recognition to, Northern Ireland as a political entity.[86]

On the political front a Constitution that laid claim to the territory of Northern Ireland was approved in the South – a claim that inevitably increased the underlying mutual mistrust, animosity and antagonism. The next generation of unionists would argue that, during the second and third quarters of the century, they had heard or seen little in the words or actions either of the hierarchy or of political leaders in the South, to persuade them that their own attitude and approach might no longer be relevant or appropriate and should change.

Most unionists come from a Protestant background, and even today (irrespective of whether they regularly, seldom, or never go to church) most of them would still call themselves Protestants. There is little doubt that their 'siege mentality', developed over several centuries, was reinforced as they watched the numbers of their co-religionists in the South decline dramatically. Many southern Protestants felt they had to emigrate and some relocated in the North. In 1920 there were approximately 50,000 Presbyterians in what is now the Republic of Ireland, but fewer than 13,500 in 1993.[87] Figures such as these pose pertinent and valid questions which, until relatively recently, had never been addressed seriously, let alone answered satisfactorily.

It should be noted that some of these issues have now been discussed in public – albeit in somewhat broad and rather general terms – in the Forum for Peace and Reconciliation, meeting in Dublin in 1995, some twenty-five years after the start of the current troubles. If followed up and positive steps taken to deal with the causes of the situation, this may eventually lead to better understanding. Moreover, in the last quarter of the century there have been important changes in the South, both in the attitude and influence of the church and in the approach and legislation of the state. Though the significance of these has not yet been fully appreciated by the majority community in the North, they may favourably affect attitudes and relationships in the future.

In the event, however, repetitive rhetoric and sporadic violence down the years since the partition of the island, evoked a defiant, almost monotonously predictable response from traditional unionist politicians, and ensured that the constitutional position of Northern Ireland and the link with Britain remained all-important to unionists as a whole. As a result, inadequate attention was paid to the concerns of nationalists, who by the late 1960s had become increasingly aware of the power of civil rights agitation. Regrettably, but perhaps not surprisingly given the history of the island, peaceful protest by the many progressed through civil commotion by more assertive activists to vicious violence by the few.

The Present Troubles
Thus began a quarter of a century of sustained terrorist activity. The events of those years have been catalogued by Paul Bew, Professor of Irish Politics, and Gordon Gillespie, researcher, both of Queen's University, Belfast, in their compact but comprehensive account *Northern Ireland – A Chronology of the Troubles 1968-1993*. Their book is essential reading for anyone wishing to study the course of 'the troubles' in Northern Ireland. It also notes the major historical splits in republicanism, such as the breakaway of the Provisional IRA (the main republican terrorist organisation, hereafter referred to simply as the IRA) from the Official IRA, and the emergence of some of the other republican terrorist factions, as well as the formation of most of the so-called 'loyalist' paramilitary groups.

However, the venom and virulence of the men of violence on both sides; the rancour and resentment engendered by them; the murder and maiming of the victims; the hurt and heartache of the bereaved; all these facets of the current troubles are still too much a part of the present for a cool, constructive or balanced analysis of those grim times to be made in a short survey such as this. Moreover, any summary can only be selective. Hence the years of the troubles, though they have left a legacy of sorrow and suffering to thousands, and adversely affected the lives of most people in the province in one way or another, are not dealt with in detail here. Nevertheless, it is possible to identify old historical attitudes, perceptions and reactions (or some variant of them) in recent events, and factors such as these – attitudes towards people, reactions against their beliefs and behaviour, and perceptions about their intentions – may still play a part in determining how one group interacts with another. Indeed, if recognised as stumbling-blocks to peaceful co-existence and faced up to, they may possibly be addressed.

Despite three decades of turmoil, most of the people of Northern Ireland have clung to the hope that things might improve. Ultimately, however, the future of the province as a whole depends on the attitude and approach of the two communities; an acceptance that nationalists and unionists alike must share the same small patch of land that they each regard as home; a realisation that in the long term the good of each community relies to a considerable extent on the goodwill of the other, and on the common good of both; a determination to avoid gratuitous provocation of, or political point scoring against the other side; and a definite resolve to try and understand the other tradition and actively establish trust.

Conditioned by the conflicts and concerns of yesterday, the Ulster-Scots (and those of Anglo-Irish stock and others in the wider unionist community who wish, like most of them, to retain their British identity) have become Ulstermen of today. As such they, together with their neighbours and fellow Ulstermen who perceive themselves as Irish rather than British, must face not only the risks and the realities, the crises and the certainties of today, but also the changes and challenges of tomorrow.

APPENDIX TO PART ONE

The Scotch-Irish in America:
A Short Summary

The Name

Professor J. G. Leyburn, in an Appendix to *The Scotch-Irish – A Social History*, discusses the use of the term 'Scotch-Irish'.[88] He notes that Francis Makemie (who emigrated in 1683 from Ulster to Maryland, and today is regarded as the father of Presbyterianism in America) was described in the enrolment register for 1675 in the University of Glasgow as *Scoto-Hybernicus*. He also mentions that in 1695 the Secretary of Maryland reported that 'the Scotch-Irish are numerous' in two counties of the colony, and quotes two Anglican clergymen who in 1723 referred to settlers from Ireland who 'call themselves Scotch-Irish'. One went on to specify that they were from the north of Ireland, the other to describe them as 'the bitterest railers against the church that ever trod upon American ground'! (They evidently had brought their resentment against the Test Act and the Anglican Establishment to America.) Although they were often loosely referred to as 'Irish', it is clear that the name 'Scotch-Irish' was coined at least 300 years ago, and was being used (on occasion at least) by the time their main migration began. In recent years authors from Britain and Ireland have tended to use the modern variant 'Scots-Irish', though the original may more accurately reflect the historical context. In this Appendix the more traditional 'Scotch-Irish' appellation has therefore been retained in contemporary quotations, while elsewhere in the text the modern 'Scots-Irish' form has been adopted. The more specific term 'Ulster-Scots' is probably preferred today by the descendants of those seventeenth century (predominantly lowland and Presbyterian) Scots planters who never made the second migration across the

Atlantic, but remained in the north of Ireland. It has therefore been used in the sub-title of the study, throughout the overview of their history in Chapter II, and in subsequent chapters which pertain to their present problems in Northern Ireland.

The Migration from Ulster

The main exodus of the Scots-Irish from Ulster to America between 1717 and 1775 has been called 'The Great Migration'. Leyburn describes five major waves of migration during these years, and relates them to specific precipitating causal events in the north of Ireland, such as a spate of lapsing leases and evictions, or consecutive years of drought and poor crops. These were superimposed on a background of civil and religious, social and economic disadvantage. It is likely that upwards of 200,000 left Ulster for the American colonies in the six decades before the Revolutionary War.[89]

The later and numerically much larger exodus of (predominantly Roman Catholic) Irish from the island of Ireland as a whole, which peaked during and after the Great Famine of 1845-49, is outwith the scope of this limited summary and is not discussed here. Nor is the direct migration of Scots from Scotland to the New World referred to at all – except where it overlaps with the story of the Scots-Irish from Ulster. Although a majority of such Scots settled in Canada, and the influx of Scots-Irish outstripped that of Scots into colonial America, there were some very significant Scottish settlements in the American colonies.

Groups of Scots began to arrive in New Jersey in the late seventeenth century. In 1746 they founded the College of New Jersey at Princeton as a Presbyterian institution for the training of their ministers.[90] Although comparatively few Scots-Irish actually settled in New Jersey, many from other middle and southern colonies benefited greatly from the educational facilities provided at Princeton. In those early days the College was a centre that helped to supply ministers for more isolated congregations of Scots-Irish Presbyterians throughout frontier and back-country areas, and provided many young men from these outlying regions with the opportunity for higher education.

Highland Scots had begun to arrive in North Carolina in the late 1720s, and were encouraged to settle in the colony during the governorship (1734-51) of Gabriel Johnston from Dumfries. It was only after the '45 rebellion and the defeat of Bonnie Prince Charlie at the battle of Culloden in 1746, however, that they did so in significant numbers. By the time of the Revolutionary War, most Scots and many Scots-Irish in the Carolinas were loyalist.[91] They fought for the British, and at the major battles of Cowpens and King's Mountain, clashed with Scots-Irish patriots.

Frontier Settlements
Throughout the period of their main migration, relatively few Ulster immigrants (apart from indentured servants) remained long in the eastern coastal regions after disembarkation. Most headed west toward the frontier, after equipping themselves as best they could for the journey and for starting work on their future homes and their allocated lands. Those arriving with the first two migratory waves settled initially in Pennsylvania, while those arriving in the early 1740s (as well as the younger sons of those already settled in the more developed areas of that colony) overflowed southward along the Shenandoah Valley into Virginia. By the late 1740s significant numbers of Scots-Irish were settling the Piedmont country of North Carolina, supplemented in 1754 and 1755 by fresh arrivals with the fourth great wave from Ulster. Indian raids delayed the effective settlement of the Piedmont area of South Carolina until the mid-1760s. Undoubtedly some Scots-Irish pushed further west across the mountains despite the fact that all territory west of the Appalachians was designated an Indian Reserve by royal declaration in 1763. It was only after the Revolutionary War, however, that they moved in substantial numbers into Kentucky and Tennessee. Germans (initially from small, rather exclusive pietist sects, though later mainly Lutherans) constituted the other major group of immigrants ever seeking new lands. The pioneers of the various national groups, however, tended to keep their early settlements separate from each other.[92]

A Buffer Zone

The Provincial Assembly in Pennsylvania was Quaker dominated and had from the outset endeavoured to establish and maintain their dealings with the Indians on a peaceful and friendly basis. While 'native American' is the politically correct term today – and Quakers and early Pietists alike would probably have approved wholeheartedly of this more accurate, acceptable and inclusive nomenclature – they were known then as Indians. So to better portray the historical connotations of ignorance and fear, prejudice and exploitation that dogged them in their own land until comparatively recent times, and without any intent or implication of disrespect now, the old name has been retained in this summary.

Although administrators in other colonies may have been less scrupulous, Quaker officials in Pennsylvania had always been meticulous about purchasing Indian land at a fair price before allocating it for settlement. Yet as early as 1720, James Logan, a Quaker from Ulster and Provincial Secretary at the time, was apparently apprehensive about the potential Indian menace. He suggested that 'it might be prudent to plant a Settlement of such men as those who formerly had so bravely defended Derry and Inniskillen as a frontier in case of any Disturbance'. Within a decade, however, he was to complain that a settlement of five families of fellow-countrymen from the north of Ireland gave him more trouble than fifty of any other people![93]

Fear on the Frontier

During the early, comparatively peaceful days of the first half of the century, their impatience and impetuosity often made the Scots-Irish 'troublesome settlers to the government and hard neighbours to the Indian'. The Quaker régime in Pennsylvania was frequently exasperated by their disregard for legal formalities and their habit of squatting on any available uninhabited land. Later, their bravery and their inherent stubbornness gained for the Scots-Irish a reputation as formidable frontier

fighters, particularly in the dangerous and deteriorating situation that developed in the 1750s and 60s, during the Seven Years
War and Pontiac's War. The latter was a wholly Indian reaction
to the relentless advance of the settlers, but Indians had also
been drawn into the former, even though it was essentially a
conflict between Britain and France (and other European nations). Indeed, because of the frequency and ferocity of French-
incited Indian raids along the whole frontier region, it is known
in America as the French and Indian War.

Thus while British redcoats fought in the major battles, it was
largely Scots-Irish settlers who bore the brunt of the guerrilla-
type struggle with the Indians, quickly learning to fight as their
enemies fought. They suffered terribly, but retaliated in kind
and just as terribly. On the other hand, some of the pietistic or
more pacific groups of Germans would withdraw rather than
fight Indians. At all events, migration from both Ulster and
Germany virtually ceased during these years. Though Indian
raids continued for some time, migration from Ulster resumed
when the wars officially ended, and reached a peak in the four
years before the Revolutionary War. By then the Scots-Irish had
become the largest ethnic group along the frontier region of
Pennsylvania, Virginia and the Carolinas.[94]

Rumblings of Revolution
The Scots-Irish were generally enthusiastic and ardent supporters of the patriot cause, especially in Virginia and Pennsylvania.
Here, in 1774 at Hanover, Lancaster County, and in 1775 at
Hanna's Town, Westmoreland County, largely Scots-Irish communities adopted declarations in which they condemned oppressive actions of the Parliament of Great Britain, and resolved
to oppose them. Both events occurred more than a year before
the official Declaration of Independence was agreed. (Hanna's
Town, a log-cabin settlement founded by a Robert Hanna from
Ulster, boasted one of the most westerly courthouses of the colonial period. In 1782, it was attacked and burned by an Indian
war-party, having been targeted by the British, whose agents –

following the example of the French of an earlier generation – recruited and encouraged Indians to carry out such raids.)[95]

However, further south in the Piedmont country of the Carolinas, Scots-Irish enthusiasm for rebellion was, by and large, only lukewarm. Here (for very different reasons in North Carolina and South Carolina) many back-country settlers had become alienated from the earlier established colonists of the Tidewater coastal areas. Thus some were disinclined initially to help their eastern neighbours in their struggle against the British. Yet even here there were pockets of staunch support for the patriot cause, as in Mecklenburg County, where the predominantly Scots-Irish militia companies declared for independence in 1775 – again well before the Declaration of Independence was approved by the Continental Congress meeting in Philadelphia in July 1776.[96]

The Declaration of Independence
'The top tier of Revolutionary philosophers and propagandists was made up of the quartet of the three Virginians, Thomas Jefferson, James Madison and Patrick Henry, and the Englishman Thomas Paine, but the second tier consisted of Scots-Irish Revolutionary committee men like Thomas McKean, Charles Thompson and James Smith'. In his book, *God's Frontiersmen – the Scots-Irish Epic*, Rory Fitzpatrick writes of the important behind-the-scenes role of such men in sowing the seeds of the struggle for independence. All three of those mentioned above were signatories of the Declaration of Independence, and all had been students of Francis Allison, who had emigrated from Ulster to Pennsylvania, and established a school at New London. There he had faithfully passed on the radical ideas that would underpin and justify the concept of revolution – ideas he had learned as a student in Glasgow from another Ulsterman, Francis Hutcheson, who was one of the great philosophers of his age.[97]

Charles Thompson was the Ulster-born, hard-working, long-serving Secretary of the Continental Congress, who wrote out the first draft of the Declaration of Independence, before the prose was perfected by Thomas Jefferson and his committee in 1776. (He later designed the original Great Seal of the United States of America.) John Hancock, from a Scots-Irish family, was President of the Congress at the time, and the first to sign the Declaration – in deliberately bold, large letters that King George III (who was reputed to have poor vision) could read! The first printing of the Declaration was by yet another immigrant from Ulster, John Dunlap.[98]

Trials and Triumphs of War

That the Scots-Irish played a significant part in the Revolutionary War itself is attested by much contemporary evidence. For example, Joseph Galloway, a lawyer and former delegate to the Continental Congress, and also Major-General Robertson, a British officer, are both reported as having told a Committee of the House of Commons that they made up about half the troops in the Continental Army. In 1778, Johann Heindrick, a Hessian officer serving with the British forces, wrote, 'Call this war by whatever name you may, only call it not an American rebellion; it is nothing more or less than a Scotch-Irish Presbyterian rebellion.'

Others have asserted that Scots-Irish predominated in the rank and file of the famous Pennsylvania Line, that they formed the backbone of George Washington's army, and that during the dreadful winter of 1777-78 at Valley Forge, when others deserted him, they remained resolute, despite the dire conditions. Washington himself is credited with the tribute, 'If defeated everywhere else, I shall make my last stand for liberty among the Scotch-Irish of my native Virginia.' Among his generals were a number of Ulster stock – Daniel Morgan, John Stark, Anthony Wayne, and Henry Knox, his Chief of Artillery, to name but a few.[99]

Morgan, though not in command of the forces involved in the first major American victory of the war at Saratoga, had led a detachment of Virginian riflemen in the battle, after which the defeated General Burgoyne paid him the compliment, 'Your

Scotch-Irish rifles are the finest in the world.' Early in 1781, and on this occasion in command at Cowpens, in the southern sector, he urged his frontiersmen to 'Look for the epaulets! Pick off the epaulets!' As before, their superior marksmanship was a decisive factor in winning the day.

A few months earlier at nearby King's Mountain, another battle had been fought and won by a force made up largely of Scots-Irish over-mountain men, led by a Presbyterian elder, Colonel William Campbell, several of whose senior officers were also elders. They had been sent off to battle by one of their ministers, the Rev Samuel Doak, with the emotive exhortation (in the words of the Old Testament battle-cry) to take up 'the sword of the Lord and of Gideon'. The less lofty and more down to earth, but equally stirring command of their elder-leader, was to 'shout like hell and fight like devils'. Following these two battles the (initially successful) southern campaign of the British commander, Lord Cornwallis, faltered and failed to regain momentum. Indeed, they heralded the end of the war for Britain.[100]

The Winning of the West
The 'winning of the west' began in the 1780s, after the War of Independence ended, and Presbyterian Scots-Irish pioneers were in the van of a new westward surge of settlers through the former frontier regions of Pennsylvania, Virginia, and the Carolinas, into Ohio, Kentucky and Tennessee and beyond. However, it was here, to the west of the Appalachians, that great numbers of people of many different national backgrounds and characteristics now met and merged, intermixed and intermarried, as had not happened to the east of the mountains.

Here too, religious affiliations were affected by changing circumstances. Even in the old colonial period, the traditional Presbyterian insistence on a well educated, highly trained ministry, had from time to time resulted in the supply of ministers failing to meet the needs of the Scots-Irish frontier settlements. Now as the west opened up and new settlers spread out, the shortage of trained ministers was exacerbated. This, together

with the greater availability of (possibly less academically qualified, though undoubtedly zealous, enthusiastic and energetic)
pastors of other denominations, and the added attraction and
appeal of less austere and more contemporary forms of worship,
led many Scots-Irish to join other churches. It was at this time
also that their story as a distinctive group gradually came to a
close. It was as fully-fledged and integrated Americans, rather
than 'Scotch-Irish', that they moved west with other Americans
to settle and possess the whole land.[101]

Great Americans
Having integrated so completely as Americans, the name of the
'Scotch-Irish' as a distinctive group almost disappeared from
use in the years following the Revolutionary War. Irish Americans,
whose much larger migration began during the Great Famine in
the next century, apparently claimed that it 'was revived and
then enthusiastically adopted after 1850 solely because of
prejudice'. Professor Leyburn, in Appendix I of his well-known
social history of the 'Scotch-Irish', concedes that the point seems
well taken.[102] Such overt anti-Catholic and anti-Irish prejudice
has long since disappeared from American society, and today
Irish Americans form a large and very influential group.
According to Rory Fitzpatrick 'the Mountain Men and the mil-
lionaires, the politicians and the frontiersmen are remembered
because they are part of American mythology'. However, 'the
great mass of middle-class Scots-Irish who contributed so much
in the nineteenth century are long forgotten,' and 'public aware-
ness of the Ulster Scots [sic] as an ethnic group has also gone.'[103]
Nevertheless, although they may have 'lost their identity as a
separate people'[104] in a way that the Amish – and other immigrant groups including the Irish Americans of today – possibly
have not, from time to time individual Americans of Scots-Irish
stock have played a leading role in the history of their country.
    Names such as Davy Crockett and Sam Houston,[105] are familiar
to all Americans, as also are those of Civil War generals such as
Ulysses Grant and Stonewall Jackson,[106] and successful business

families like Getty and Mellon.[107] These, together with the names of some thirteen Presidents – including Andrew Jackson, James Buchanan and Chester Alan Arthur (the only first generation Presidents) in the nineteenth century, Woodrow Wilson in the first quarter of the twentieth century, and Richard Nixon, Jimmy Carter and Bill Clinton in the second half – provide some indication of the part descendants of Scots-Irish immigrants from the small province of Ulster have played in the story of the great nation of the United States of America.[108]

PART TWO

A Background to the Present

CHAPTER THREE

The Ulster-Scots Today

Conditioned by Circumstances – Religious and Political
Much has been said and written in the past about the 'frontier spirit' of 'Scotch-Irish' emigrants, or the adaptability and entrepreneurial energy of the Ulster-Scots abroad; or about the Protestant 'work ethic', the pride of the Ulsterman in his reputation for reliability, and the quality of his work – whether ships or linen. Be that as it may, and regardless of the validity of such assertions or assumptions in the past, they are inappropriate and possibly irrelevant today. Not only have the shipbuilding industry and the linen business declined drastically, but the introduction of the National Health Service and Social Security benefits, and the wider availability of secondary and tertiary education, have led to a greater reliance upon rights, rather than on personal effort and responsibility. The future lies in equal rights and equal opportunities for all, regardless of colour, creed, or culture, and this is as it should be – though in the absence of any basic concept of personal responsibility, available rights and opportunities will always be subject to abuse by greedy and self-centred individuals of whatever religious persuasion or political allegiance. The moral and spiritual aspects of religion are of less concern to most people today than formerly. Nevertheless, religious and political factors, whether based on personal conviction or not, still influence life in the two main communities in Northern Ireland, to the extent that background factors such as these have to be considered in any attempt to explain or understand the attitudes of any group today.

Most of the early Scots settlers in Ulster were Presbyterians, and Presbyterianism has helped to give successive generations of their descendants their identity. For those with an interest in church history, *Our Irish Presbyterian Heritage* and *The Presbyterian Church in Ireland: A Popular History*, by the Very Rev Professor Finlay Holmes merit special mention and study. The first presbytery in Ulster was formed in 1642 by the chaplains and officer-elders of Monro's Scottish army, and soon fifteen congregations in south Antrim and north Down had applied for membership. By the end of the seventeenth century the original presbytery had become the Synod of Ulster with five presbyteries. However, Presbyterianism in Ireland, as in Scotland, has been prone to schism on issues of practice, principle and doctrine. In the eighteenth century Scottish Presbyterian schismatics, Seceders and Covenanters, formed congregations and presbyteries in Ulster. The Seceders, who organised their own Secession Synod in 1818, united with the Synod of Ulster in 1840 to form the Presbyterian Church in Ireland, which included congregations and presbyteries in the south of Ireland. Currently there are five synods, one of which, with its three constituent presbyteries, covers the Republic. The Covenanters, however, always remained a separate body, known today as the Reformed Presbyterian Church. The Non-subscribing Presbyterian Church was formed following the union in the first half of the nineteenth century of those groups that had broken with the main body of Presbyterians at one time or another over subscription to the Westminster Confession of Faith. Other churches, such as the Evangelical Presbyterian Church and the Free Presbyterian Church, both distinct from the main Presbyterian Church in Ireland, have also been founded following differences that surfaced in the twentieth century.

Yet, despite the divisions of the past and the dwindling numbers of today, the Presbyterian Church in Ireland (PCI) is still the largest, not only of those churches calling themselves Presbyterian, but of all the Protestant churches in Northern Ireland. In terms of numbers throughout the whole island of Ireland, it comes third to the Roman Catholic Church (which is by far the largest) and the Church of Ireland. For a frank explanation and critical self-examination of mainstream Presbyterianism in Ireland, in the context of the on-going troubles, *A Precarious Belonging – Presbyterians and the Conflict in Ireland* by former Moderator of the General Assembly of the PCI, the Very Rev Dr John Dunlop, is well worth study by anyone attempting to understand the complexities of the current problems in Northern Ireland – including politicians, commentators and reporters.

Mention has already been made of the discrimination experienced by Presbyterians, as Dissenters, and by Roman Catholics, during the days of the Anglican Ascendancy. Nevertheless, apart from the 1798 Rebellion, Presbyterians usually stood alongside their fellow Protestants of the Anglican tradition in times of crisis and danger. The removal of religious grievances, such as the payment of tithes to the established Church of Ireland and the disestablishment of that church in the nineteenth century, together with a shared interest in charitable and other church-related activities, has drawn the mainstream Protestant churches closer together – if not those churches that are more rigidly fundamentalist in doctrine, or exclusive in practice. The PCI, the Church of Ireland, and the Methodist Church co-operate happily in many activities at central, congregational and community level.

However, some Protestant groups, and in particular the Free Presbyterian Church, led by the Rev Ian Paisley since its foundation in 1951, are often highly critical of the PCI and other mainline Protestant denominations, on the grounds that they do not hold fast enough to the fundamental doctrines of the Reformation, or are involved in some way or other in 'ecumenism' – regarded by many Ulster Protestants as a betrayal of their heritage. Moreover, the spokesmen of these larger churches have possibly been more restrained and less outspoken in any statements they may have issued against government policies with which they were unhappy. Although frequently accused of not giving specific and unambiguous Christian guidance to their people, the leaders of those mainstream churches mentioned above have consistently and publicly, repeatedly and earnestly urged them to keep the law at all times – particularly during parades and protests – and to pray and work for peace and reconciliation. From time to time, together with the Primate of the Roman Catholic Church in Ireland, they have issued an appropriate joint message to all the people of the province.

In 1994, the General Assembly of the PCI adopted *The Church's Peace Vocation*, which was subsequently published and made available to all Presbyterian congregations throughout the country. Traditional or conventional Presbyterians are often regarded as dour and their form of worship dull and dreary. Nevertheless, this short statement is one of the most idealistic and inspiring, while at the same time practical and responsible declarations of purpose and commitment to be issued by any organisation, secular or religious, to its members in the current situation. (See Appendix to Part Two.)

The combination of secularism, materialism and apathy is considered by many to be a major cause of the significant decline in attendance and support that affects all the main churches today, whether Protestant or Catholic. It is also arguably a greater threat to the church as a whole than the perceived errors or shortcomings of any particular branch of it. Yet in June 1999, a significant majority (224 to 144, with 96 registering their dissent) in the General Assembly of the PCI felt unable to approve the proposed constitution for a new Conference of Churches in Ireland, in which the Roman Catholic Church would play a very structured and prominent part. This decision is unlikely to result in the severing of those contacts that have already been established, or the withdrawal of ongoing co-operation with other main churches through existing bodies such as the Irish Council of Churches. It does demonstrate, however, the underlying strength of opinion against compromising the basic articles of the church's reformed faith by a commitment to any official or formal linkage with another church, some of whose doctrines are perceived as fundamentally flawed.

Doctrinal issues are outwith the scope of this study, and are only referred to insofar as they affect current attitudes and approaches. The Protestant emphasis on 'faith alone' as the means of salvation, and 'scripture alone' as the basis for belief, focuses the attention of the individual on the importance of personal choice rather than on the authority or tradition of any church. This highly prized freedom of choice in religious matters, established during the Reformation, and exercised through the study and interpretation of the Bible for oneself, has nevertheless contributed to the subsequent splits in Protestantism. Today, the mainstream Protestant churches in Ireland are identified as much by variations in their form of worship or of church government, as by significant differences in doctrine. Nevertheless, within these churches, labels such as 'evangelical' or 'liberal' may be bandied around about certain groups or people, and the membership of individual congregations may include individuals or groups whose views on certain aspects of core Christian belief not infrequently differ to a degree.

Differences of this type are not such a feature in those Protestant denominations – such as Baptists and Pentecostals, for example – which, because of certain distinctive beliefs or particular practices, attract mainly like-minded believers to the church. (In Northern Ireland the two specifically cited above are not generally referred to as mainstream, though in Britain and America they are relatively much stronger.) There are numerous 'special emphasis' church groups in the province, some of them very small, some that attract large congregations, and some that could best be described as 'fundamentalist' or possibly 'exclusive'.

Apart from church-related bodies, a number of groups, made up of individuals from a variety of church backgrounds, have also been actively engaged in working for peace, justice and reconciliation. Evangelical Contribution On Northern Ireland (ECONI) – a broad coalition of evangelical Christians from throughout the Protestant churches in the province – is one such group. For more than a decade, ECONI has sought 'to understand and apply biblical principles and perspectives to the situation in Northern Ireland'. Its primary purpose is 'to address evangelical Christians in order to facilitate a continuing process of engaging with God's Word and the hurts facing our divided community'. Its goal is 'to promote reflection and debate and to encourage change in values and attitudes which will lead to evangelicals being active as makers of peace and agents of healing'. Over the years it has produced a number of thought-provoking and helpful pamphlets that have considered issues such as culture and identity, repentance and reconciliation, truth and trust, and justice and mercy.

Such publications, and a number of insightful books by astute and judicious Protestant writers – if read and considered seriously by the public at large, including Catholics/nationalists as well as Protestants/unionists – might go some way towards repairing relationships between the two communities. The study by Presbyterian Minister, John Dunlop, has already been referred to, and is relevant in this context. So too are the challenging works by Church of Ireland Rector, Timothy Kinahan, *Where do we go from here? – Protestants and the Future of Northern Ireland*, and *A More Excellent Way – A Vision for Northern Ireland*.

Unfortunately, because more people watch television news reports than read books such as these, public opinion in both traditions is shaped largely by the media soundbites of politicians – often directed specifically at their own constituency, but interpreted selectively by their opponents. Sensational and sweeping assertions by republican political leaders, made in front of the world's media, that they were being excluded from power not just because of their politics but because of their religion, were both unhelpful and untrue. Such statements are also highly emotive and offensive, and likely to be counter-productive. It is ironic that the most publicised of these allegations was made just before a local newspaper (*News Letter* 14-15 July 1999) reported and commented on the results of their latest poll (conducted by Ulster Marketing Services) which suggested that a clear majority of Protestants supported power-sharing.

Terms such as 'evangelical' and 'fundamentalist' (in the original conservative Christian context) have caused considerable confusion and misunderstanding in some circles. There are those who can see no significant difference; those who suggest that while all fundamentalists are evangelicals, not all evangelicals are fundamentalists; and those who emphasise the differences, especially in attitude and approach. As indicated above, doctrinal or theological issues, though they may merit mention when considering the different attitudes of various Protestant groups, are not discussed in detail in this study. Readers interested in such matters are referred to the relevant explanatory passages in Christopher Catherwood's short but informative paperback *Crash Course on Church History*.[109]

Reference has already been made to the Protestant emphasis on 'scripture alone'. As John Dunlop has written, 'The Word of God is central to Presbyterian thinking ... Theology is tested against the Word of God and preaching is based upon the scriptures ... This careful attention to words, their meanings and their implications leads to documents being written and read carefully. Presbyterians do not live easily with studied ambiguity.' Later in the same chapter, he comments, 'They are suspicious of a culture which gives a greater priority to maintaining relationships than to being absolutely honest.'[110] Many northern Protestants either come from such a background or have to some extent been influenced by it. Whether they are active church members or no longer attend any church, whether they believe the Bible to be the Word of God or not, most are probably still instinctively wary of any attempt to fudge or obscure the meaning or the implications of the actual words used in any specific situation – be it in a private and personal, or in a public or political context.

The failure to appreciate this particular and possibly troublesome trait, this aversion to ambiguity or equivocation, has had a direct bearing on some of the difficulties that have bedevilled political progress in the province. The IRA, in their published statements, and republican spokespersons in television appearances, have shown themselves to be past masters at giving equivocal or evasive answers to awkward questions. Often what they do not say is as important as what they do say. They are apparently unconcerned if their words are interpreted naïvely or uncritically by their own constituents or by those who want to believe them.[111] At best, such assiduous ambiguity makes meaningful discussion with republicans difficult for those unionists who are willing to negotiate; at worst, it deepens mistrust in an uneasy majority community and may result in the rejection of moderates as leaders. Some outspoken unionists have described various republican media statements less charitably as 'weasel words' – with the insinuation that they may be intentionally misleading.

No discussion about Protestants in Northern Ireland would be complete without at least some reference to the Orange Order. Most Roman Catholics perceive, and the media generally portray, the Loyal Institutions such as the Orange Order, the Royal Black Institution or the Apprentice Boys of Derry as 'Protestant' organisations. They are, but only in the sense that their membership is Protestant – they are not a necessary or integral part of any Protestant denomination, nor are they subject to the jurisdiction of any Protestant church body, such as the General Assembly of the PCI, or the General Synod of the Church of Ireland. Nevertheless, they may from time to time parade to a service of worship in a Protestant church, though always with the permission of, if not at the invitation of, the appropriate authority at the local congregational level.

Some indication of how the Loyal Institutions view themselves, and of what they consider their roles to be, may be found in Chapter 3 of the Report (published in January 1997) of the Independent Review of Parades and Marches. The relevant sections are based largely on the submissions of the parading organisations to the Review. The Orange Order is the largest of these organisations, and sees itself as fulfilling a number of roles – political and social, as well as religious and cultural. Parades, many of which are held annually by the various Loyal Orders during the 'marching season' in July and August, are regarded as an integral part of their community's cultural tradition and heritage. While only a minority of Protestants (according to one estimate 25% of males over 16 years of age) may be actual members, the influence of the Orange Order – and the other Loyal Institutions – is considerable, with 86% of Protestants (in a survey commissioned for the Independent Review) sympathetic to their concerns.

The office bearers of the Loyal Institutions have in the past maintained that the parades and the routes are 'traditional', and claim the 'right' to walk the Queen's highway, pointing out that over 90% of such marches pass off without any trouble. They insist that their parades are not intended to be offensive or triumphalist, but seemingly disregard the demographic changes that have occurred in some areas over a number of decades. For example a main road, where once a parade by one of the Loyal Orders would have caused no confrontation, may today pass through a district that, over the years, has become a largely Catholic residential area. The leaders of the Orange Order point out that *The Qualifications of an Orangeman* stipulate that though he is required to 'defend the Protestant religion', an Orangeman should ever abstain 'from all uncharitable words, actions, or sentiments, towards his Roman Catholic brethren'.

Regrettably, human nature being what it is, these criteria are not always adhered to by all those associated with the marches, especially when taunts are exchanged, tempers flare, tension rises and trouble breaks out. It must be stated, however, that Orange Order leaders maintain that protesters, hangers-on, or on occasion bandsmen, who generally are not members of the Order, are responsible for most untoward incidents. Their critics, concentrating on the phraseology of other sections of the above-mentioned document, denounce it as insensitive and inflammatory, and dismiss the Orange Order itself as bigoted and sectarian. On the other hand, and possibly unexpectedly, *The Faithful Tribe – An Intimate Portrait of the Loyal Institutions* by Ruth Dudley Edwards (who incidentally comes from a southern Irish Catholic background) is a more sympathetic and positive appraisal of these organisations. It is a well-researched study, and has been described in a review by Kevin Myers, a respected and reliable southern Irish journalist, as 'one of the wisest and most perceptive books to have emerged from Northern Ireland's troubles'.[112]

According to the evidence submitted to the 1997 Independent Review, the membership of the Orange Order at that time was 70-75,000, though in a more recent television report it was suggested that membership had risen to nearer 100,000 by July 1999. Since that Review, considerable concern and dismay has been expressed in broadly unionist/Protestant circles regarding the violence that occurred in various parts of the province during the 1998 marching season. Such concern cannot be quantified or analysed accurately, and has to be balanced against other factors, such as the more recently reported rise in membership, the tense situation that arose out of the pressure of imposed deadlines in the run-up to and during the 1999 marching season, and the responsibility, restraint and discipline displayed by the Order on that occasion.

Before leaving the specific topic of the religious background of northern Protestants, the wider subject of bigotry merits some discussion, in addition to any implicit references already made to it. It is wider because it involves both Catholics and Protestants, and encompasses politics as well as religion. The *Chambers 21st Century Dictionary* defines a bigot as 'one who is persistently prejudiced, especially about religion and politics, and refuses to tolerate the opinion of others'. Protestant churches and Orange halls have been burned, as well as Roman Catholic chapels. Throughout the troubles people on both sides have been murdered because of their religion or their politics or both. In the past, Catholics have been murdered coming out of church, and Protestants murdered in church, and even since the peace process began, tit-for-tat or revenge killings by both sides have occurred all too often.

While there is no denying that there are Protestant and unionist bigots, there are also Catholic and republican bigots. Spurious cover names, such as 'Catholic Reaction Force' or 'Orange Volunteers', with direct or indirect religious connotations, have been used, or are being used, by overtly bigoted people – criminals, paramilitaries, terrorists of both traditions, call them what you will. Others who consider themselves to be ordinary decent law-abiding people, Protestant and Catholic alike, regularly repudiate the foul deeds done in their name. Yet the terrible terminology of the troubles – at best euphemistic, at worst obscene – has been accepted as part and parcel of life in our province. Terms such as 'legitimate targets', or 'mistaken identity', may be intended to prove a point or explain away or justify a murder. In actual fact they are a stark record of the ultimate in bigotry, the callous removal of that greatest of human rights, the right to life itself.

Doubts and Divisions in the Wider Majority Community
Although no longer identifiable on the basis of church attendance, membership or even nominal religious affiliation, Ulster-Scots today are still probably the largest component in the wider majority community, and traits of their dissenting tradition have undoubtedly left their imprint on the character of the province. Over the years, however, they have become an integral part of that community, the political outlook of whose members (irrespective of which church, if any, they belong to, or where their ancestors originated) is still basically unionist – of whatever shade of opinion, whether at the extremist hardline limit of the political spectrum, or at the most moderate and inclusive end.

In the past the threat of republican terrorist activity usually provoked a fairly united unionist response. Today, the Protestant/unionist community is deeply divided within itself – not so much on basic issues such as civil and religious liberty, or on constitutional concerns such as the Union with Great Britain, over all of which there is little if any internal controversy, but rather on how to safeguard them. In the past they fought at Derry and the Boyne, or closed ranks and rallied round the 'Solemn League and Covenant' when threatened. Today, after years of murder and mayhem at the hands of republican terrorists, during which some of them reacted viciously and in kind, there is the prospect of permanent peace. The problem for most of them is whether to believe the protestations of past-terrorists-turned-politicians about the sincerity of their 'peace policy' and take the unfamiliar and undoubtedly risky path of 'trust', in the hope of securing some sort of peace in the absence of any promise or proof that it will be permanent; or whether to fall back on the standard, supposedly safer, policies of the past which, while giving relief for a period, have failed to provide any long-term respite.

On 10 April 1998, after prolonged ceasefires by the mainstream paramilitary terrorist groups (both republican and so-called loyalist) and multi-party talks, an Agreement was reached by representatives of both sides. It was endorsed by an overwhelming majority of voters in a Referendum held in both parts of the island of Ireland on 22 May, and was followed up by an election of members to a new Northern Ireland Assembly on 25 June. Many hoped that this provincial Assembly would give local people more of a say in the management of their own affairs, on the basis of power-sharing and against a background of permanent peace following the early removal of the threat of terrorism.

Safeguards were written into the Agreement to ensure that key decisions in the Assembly would be taken on a cross-community basis. Many of those who opposed the Agreement are convinced, however, (on reasonably sound estimates, but no conclusive evidence) that only a small majority of unionists voted for it. A significant minority certainly voted against it, believing that it was fatally flawed, that it had been fudged to favour nationalists and republicans, that it lacked specific safeguards for a Union that would be weakened by the repeal of existing legislation. They would maintain that it was only on the basis of assurances and pledges given by the Prime Minister that many fellow-unionists voted for it (pp. 180-181).

Those unionists who voted for the Agreement did so despite the lack of any firm or specific statement from republicans that the war was over, and regardless of repeated declarations by spokesmen for the IRA that there would be no 'decommissioning' of weapons. There is little doubt that many of them had grave misgivings and genuine reservations about issues related to justice and democracy. Nevertheless, they believed that it provided the best chance for a more peaceful future – and many still do. There is equally little doubt, however, that a significant number of such unionists have become deeply disillusioned since then – on several counts, all of which continue to concern them. They have seen those aspects of the Agreement that involved concessions to terrorism, such as the early release of prisoners, being implemented despite continuing violence – regardless of the assurances they had received. On the other hand, they have seen no movement on that section of it dealing with what has since been described as the 'obligation' of terrorists to decommission. (An opinion poll in March 1999, suggested that 14% of them had by that date changed their minds and would now vote against the Agreement). They also felt aggrieved that, after being persuaded – much against the grain – to accept a fudged form of words that would enable republicans to sign up to the Agreement, the latter had exploited the situation by insisting that the letter of that Agreement, rather than the spirit of it, must be followed. The fudge persists in the minds of many unionists, despite the statements from the IRA and their political apologists during the Mitchell Review (pp. 154-5); though 'the guns are silent', it is likely to cause concern so long as the threat of a return to violence remains.

CHAPTER FOUR

Concerns of Communities in Conflict

Polarised Politics

The politico-religious alignments and divisions in Northern Ireland are generally portrayed by the international media, and perceived by those not familiar with the province, as a rather simple arrangement of Protestant/unionist on the one side and Roman Catholic/nationalist on the other. Such a broad generalisation may be a fairly reasonable rule of thumb, but is not always applicable or appropriate, and gives but little indication of the nuances of opinion inherent in the local situation. As regards religious beliefs, while there are still a good number of God-fearing Protestants and practising Roman Catholics, an increasing number of 'nominal' church members, particularly among the younger age groups and in urban areas, have little or no time for their respective churches, and but scant knowledge or understanding of basic Christian belief. Concerning the 'polarity' of politics in the province, there is no doubt that emotive and divisive constitutional issues such as maintaining the Union with Britain or attaining a united Ireland exert a greater influence on voting habits throughout the province than do more mundane matters such as health, education or employment – issues that in other circumstances might provide common cause for concern to both communities.

There are, nevertheless, significant and sometimes bitter differences on each side between 'moderates' and 'hardliners'. (The adjective 'hardline', used below to describe some political parties, generally refers to the extremism or inflexibility of a particular party's policies; it does not necessarily indicate the party's attitude to violence, which is noted separately.) Moreover, the

approach of traditional enemies to certain problems may be surprisingly similar, as is seen in the attitudes of both hardline republican and loyalist parties to some sensitive issues. Both
groups hold the same views about the early release of terrorist
prisoners and the decommissioning of arms. Furthermore, a
strong stubborn streak – reflected in the confrontational rhetoric
of the two sides and in the many murals in both loyalist and republican areas – is common to the two traditions.

However, old slogans such as 'No Surrender' and 'Not An
Inch', and the more recent 'Ulster Says No' outcry against the
Anglo-Irish Agreement, are so closely associated with unionist
protest, that it is not altogether surprising that unionists themselves are often portrayed as invariably 'intransigent'. Ironically,
such slogans probably divert media attention away from the
equally stubborn if less strident stance of their political opponents, who have generally adopted a more subtle approach.
Though seldom described in current affairs programmes or
news reports as intransigent, the uncompromising position of
nationalists on the issues of an internal settlement and of cross-
border bodies with executive powers, and the obstinacy of the
Irish government on the Republic's territorial claim to Northern
Ireland, have in the past been manifestly intransigent. The inflexibility of republicans on the decommissioning of arms issue
– despite the smooth-talk of their spokespersons that they are
against violence – has been as great a threat to the peace process
as unionist intransigence..

The Social Democratic and Labour Party (SDLP) is the main
nationalist political party in Northern Ireland. Though not prepared to compromise on certain issues (see above) the party is
patently moderate, its attitude and approach are definitely not
extremist, and it has consistently condemned violence. Even so,
it displays at times a tendency to fudge rather than face up to issues that concern and trouble moderate unionists. Nevertheless,
the party has always been prepared to present and argue its case
in a constitutional manner in Parliament, and three of its MPs
retained their seats in the 1997 United Kingdom General

Election – the first since new constituency boundary changes were introduced. It participated fully in multi-party talks, welcomed the Agreement and campaigned for its acceptance in the Referendum. Moreover, the party won the highest number of first preference votes in the Assembly election and secured twenty-four seats in the new Northern Ireland Assembly. Arguing that decommissioning of arms is a political 'obligation' for parties linked to terrorist groups, but not a 'precondition' for inclusion in the Assembly Executive, it strongly advocated the implementation of the Agreement in full, including both the establishment of an Executive and decommissioning.

Sinn Féin, the main hardline republican party, though it now claims to be separate from the IRA, is generally regarded as the political wing of that very efficient terrorist organisation, and on this basis was barred from multi-party talks (by both the British and Irish governments) until the IRA had reinstated its broken ceasefire. In the 1997 General Election the party won two seats, but on principle their MPs, past and present, have never taken their seats in Parliament. Sinn Féin representatives, though present when the Agreement was concluded, would not formally endorse it until it had been approved by the party membership. Nevertheless, they claimed it as a stepping stone towards a united Ireland, despite the arguments of a number of traditionalists that it was a betrayal of republican ideals. Most Sinn Féin members followed the leadership line, however, and at a special Ard Fheis called to discuss the issues of the Agreement (and at the subsequent Referendum) voted overwhelmingly to accept it. The party constitution was also amended at the Ard Fheis to enable elected members to sit in the proposed Northern Ireland Assembly, and eighteen of the party's candidates were successful at the subsequent election.

Prior to 15 August 1998, when a dissident republican terrorist group planted a car-bomb in Omagh town centre, killing 29 people (the greatest number killed in any one incident), Sinn Féin leaders had always insisted that they would not indulge in 'the politics of condemnation'. While 'regretting' violence in

general terms, they had never publicly condemned that of any
republican organisation. Nevertheless, they did so on this occasion, and subsequent statements and the appointment of a Sinn
Féin representative to liaise with the Independent International
Commission on Decommissioning, prompted speculation about
a possible change in the party's attitude to violence. However, not
until November 1999, at the end of the Mitchell Review (p. 154),
did the party accept that decommissioning was an essential part
of the Agreement. Nor was there any specific suggestion, even
then, that the IRA, having repeatedly declared that it would
not decommission its weapons, might, with the appointment
of its own representative to the Commission, be about to consider the issue.

The Irish Republican Socialist Party (IRSP) and Republican
Sinn Féin are small breakaway republican parties, without MPs
or Assembly Members. Both have been opposed to any ceasefire, and are allegedly linked to the Irish National Liberation
Army (INLA) and the Continuity IRA (or Continuity Army
Council) respectively – two groups that have been responsible
for many bombings and killings since the renewed IRA ceasefire. The Real IRA is yet another dissident terrorist organisation.
Having broken away from the IRA towards the end of 1997
when the latter restored its ceasefire and Sinn Féin entered
multi-party talks, the group almost certainly has had access to
IRA bomb-making and mortar technology. It is allegedly linked
to the Thirty-Two County Sovereignty Committee, the latest
political offshoot of the republican movement. The Real IRA admitted responsibility for the Omagh bombing. Public outrage at
the atrocity led to the announcement by the group, first of a temporary suspension of their activities, then a 'complete cessation'.
Since then the INLA has also declared a ceasefire. The only dissident group not on ceasefire now is the Continuity IRA, which is
said to be attracting militant diehards who become disenchanted
with the so-called 'cessations'.

On the unionist side, the historical propensity of Protestants,
and Presbyterians in particular, for dissent, division and schism on

matters of religious principle, is paralleled on the secular stage by such a proliferation of political parties as to preclude any pretence or semblance of unionist unity – not on the concept of the Union with Britain, but on the question of how best it can be maintained. At present there are three main unionist parties with parliamentary representation, all of which are opposed to violence.

The most moderate of them, the Ulster Unionist Party (UUP) is also the largest and has ten MPs. The leadership negotiated the 1998 Good Friday Agreement and, claiming that it actually strengthened the Union, advocated its acceptance in the Referendum. Their action was endorsed by both the Executive and the Council of the party, but a number of sitting MPs publicly criticised the stance adopted by their party leader, and allegedly voted against the Agreement in the Referendum. Despite the divisions in the party, the splitting of the party vote when several members stood as independent unionists in the Assembly Election, and the demoralising effect such disunity had on its supporters, the UUP won twenty-eight seats in the new Assembly. Of those who stood as independent unionists, three were elected but they all later resigned from the UUP to form the United Unionist Assembly Party (UUAP).

The main problem for moderate unionists in general, and the UUP and its leadership in particular, is that more members may defect, for there is no doubt that frustration has been increasing in the party since the heady days of the Agreement, not only among politicians and party activists but also among rank and file supporters. Many who had voted for the Agreement in the Referendum on the basis of the Prime Minister's assurances, now feel badly let down (pp. 180-181). In view of the simmering unease, the UUP leader, having managed to persuade the party Council to defer a decision on the deal agreed at the Mitchell Review, pending possible movement on decommissioning by the IRA, cannot afford to compromise further (p. 157). Most moderate unionists find it difficult to understand why Sinn Féin, a party that now claims to have rejected violence completely, cannot call on the IRA to start to decommission – unless of course the party considers republican unity to be more important than peace.

Regarded by most media commentators as hardline, the Democratic Unionist Party (DUP) has two MPs. The party, concerned that the renewed IRA ceasefire was merely a tactical move and (in the absence of any decommissioning of arms) did not reflect a real commitment to peace, withdrew from multi-party talks when Sinn Féin was admitted to those talks on the basis of that ceasefire. Its leaders greeted the Good Friday Agreement with dismay, considering it to be seriously flawed with inadequate safeguards against unrepentant or unreconstructed terrorists. In their view the early release of terrorist prisoners, and the allocation of places on the Executive of the new Assembly, were not linked firmly enough to actual decommissioning. They also believed that the Union with Britain would be weakened rather than strengthened by the Agreement, and they campaigned passionately against it. On these issues they were joined by the United Kingdom Unionist Party (UKUP), which advocates closer integration with the rest of the United Kingdom. The UKUP's one MP had also withdrawn from the talks and now argued the case against the Agreement with legalistic precision and persuasive logic. Although the joint opposition of these parties failed to prevent acceptance of the Agreement in the decisive Referendum, in the subsequent Election the DUP won twenty seats, and the UKUP five seats on the Northern Ireland Assembly. (Later, four members of the UKUP broke away and formed the NIUP – the Northern Ireland Unionist Party). Both parties are strongly opposed to any party with terrorist links having seats on an Executive.

Two 'unionist fringe' or loyalist parties, which only began to attract media attention as talk of a peace initiative grew, have links with so-called loyalist paramilitary terrorist groups. The Ulster Democratic Party (UDP) has ties with both the Ulster Defence Association (UDA) and the Ulster Freedom Fighters (UFF), while the Progressive Unionist Party (PUP) admits to being close to the Ulster Volunteer Force (UVF) and the Red Hand Commando. From 1991-1997 the overtly paramilitary activities of these loyalist terrorist organisations were generally co-ordinated by the CLMC – the Combined Loyalist Military Command. Because the paramilitary groups with which they are linked were deemed to be on ceasefire at the time, the UDP and the PUP were admitted to the multi-party talks, at which they made significant contributions. Both parties welcomed the Agreement and actively supported its acceptance. They are still small parties, however, and have no MPs to date. While the PUP won two seats in the new Assembly, the UDP failed to win any. The attitude of these parties to decommissioning is fairly close to that of Sinn Féin, however, and the paramilitary groups with which they have links are not prepared to decommission their weapons unilaterally.

The Loyalist Volunteer Force (LVF), a small group that disagreed with the CLMC ceasefire policy, broke away in 1996. It has been responsible for many killings since then, but in May 1998, declared a ceasefire, and just before Christmas that year made a gesture towards decommissioning by handing in a few weapons – so far the only terrorist group to do so. Since late 1998 two new dissident groups, the Orange Volunteers and the Red Hand Defenders, have carried out sporadic sectarian attacks – the latter admitting to the horrific murder of a high-profile nationalist solicitor. Some suspect that the use of a powerful under-car explosive device suggests involvement by a mainstream organisation.

Other parties have attempted to break the established mould of polarised politics in the province. The Alliance Party of Northern Ireland, founded in the early days of the troubles, has always condemned violence and campaigned positively on a platform of partnership and cross-community co-operation, on matters affecting the welfare of the community rather than on emotive and divisive issues. It welcomes without reservation Protestants and Catholics alike. While in general 'accepting' the Union, the party would not call itself 'unionist' in any exclusive sense. Thus its members tend to be regarded neither as genuine Irish by dyed-in-the-wool nationalists, nor as true Brits by conventional unionists! So despite its idealism, and inclusive mem-

bership – which none of the more traditional parties even aspire
to match – to date the party has failed to attract sufficient support from a polarised electorate to make any breakthrough in
the voting patterns of the province, and has no elected MP.
Nevertheless, it engaged wholeheartedly in the multi-party
talks, strongly supported the Agreement, and won six seats at
the recent election for the new Northern Ireland Assembly. Both
the local Labour Party and the recently formed Women's
Coalition also participated in the multi-party talks and helped
secure the Good Friday Agreement. However, only the latter
party was successful in the election, winning two seats in the
Assembly.

The Two Traditions – Distrust and Division
The status and position of the political parties in the province in
late 1999 has been set out in the previous section. Mention has
also been made of some significant shifts in emphasis. It is necessary, however, at this stage to consider some of the concerns
that continue to trouble the ordinary people of the two traditions – unionist and nationalist/republican – as events have un-
folded in recent years. Although there have been a number of
noticeable changes in attitude, major differences remain, and in
the long term these cannot be glossed over in any effort, however
praiseworthy, by either government or any party to achieve
consensus, let alone reconciliation. A form of words that lacks
specificity may sustain the semblance of rapprochement for a
period, but cannot create trust or resolve fundamental disagreements.

Apart from the rhetoric and the wrangling of the politicians,
it is evident that the rights and wrongs of specific policies, decisions and incidents are perceived very differently by the two
main groups in the province. Both are concerned, almost exclusively, with their own tradition and history, their knowledge of
the other being based mainly on their own myths. Both generally
underestimate the depth of feeling underlying the very real
fears and the genuine and legitimate aspirations of the other

community. Indifference and insensitivity, misunderstanding and misrepresentation, all contribute to deepen distrust. In the historically orientated 'no surrender' culture of Ulster, a fundamental change in the mindset of both sides may well be needed to break the vicious circle. This is a difficult but not impossible goal, and will require a determined and deliberate decision by the leadership of the two sides, at both party political and local community level, to adopt a less confrontational and more positive approach in tense or potentially dangerous situations, rather than invariably indulging in the ritual recitation of the faults and failings of others.

To appreciate the depth of distrust and hostility that currently exists between the extremes of the two traditions in Northern Ireland, it is necessary to explore the concerns of both communities, and their attitudes and reactions to each other. The relationship of the communities and the political parties to both the British and the Irish governments also has to be examined; unionists are very wary of both, and republicans have always blamed the British.

Attitudes to the British and Irish Governments

Those who are unfamiliar with the nuances of the history of the province may sometimes wonder why the pro-British unionist community in Northern Ireland is so often so critical of the policies and actions of the British government – irrespective of which party is in power at the time. Unlike those of Anglo-Irish stock, most Ulster-Scots (the major component of that community) had little reason to support the establishment during their first 250 years in the country. Regarded generally as troublesome Dissenters with a reputation for independent thinking and stubbornness, they were discriminated against for generations. In the last 150 years, however, their political and other interests have tended to converge with those of other Protestants. Today, although a majority in this wider inclusive Protestant/unionist community consider themselves British, old dissenting traits and a tendency to question government motives and intentions have not entirely disappeared.

For quite a number of years, unionists as a whole – including many whose political preferences might best be described as broadly unionist, as well as those with uncompromising or hardline attitudes – have been increasingly disturbed by trends in British policy and practice in the North, which they perceive and describe as the 'slippery slope' to a united Ireland. The signing in 1985 of the Anglo-Irish Agreement, which gave a definite role in the affairs of Northern Ireland to the Irish government, was regarded by most unionists – even those at the most moderate end of the political spectrum – as an act of betrayal. Their bitter resentment at the manner in which it was imposed on them (having been drawn up without either majority consultation or consent) has not been fully appreciated by either government, British or Irish, nor appreciably assuaged by repeated reassurances from both.

Unionist attitudes to the Irish government are possibly easier to understand, having been shaped to a considerable degree by the adversarial approach adopted by successive governments in the South during the second and third quarters of the twentieth century. Since the start of the present troubles, however, significant changes have undoubtedly taken place in the Republic of Ireland, both in the attitude and legislation of the state, and in the influence and authority of the Roman Catholic Church. Reference has already been made to such matters in Chapter II. Nevertheless, the potential significance of these far-reaching changes, overshadowed as they have been by the pervading violence in Northern Ireland, has not yet been fully appreciated by any but a few of the majority unionist community in the province. Of more concern to most unionists was the repeated refusal of the Irish government in the past to consider any amendment (before an overall settlement was agreed) of Articles 2 & 3 of the Constitution of Ireland, which laid claim to the territory of Northern Ireland. This was perceived as both intransigent and unhelpful, and caused considerable resentment. Today, in the light of the overwhelming readiness of those in the Republic who voted in the 1998 Referendum to accept changes in the Constitution, including amendments to the cherished Articles (admittedly after a deal had been struck), the question has been asked by some why one of the major stumbling-blocks to possible accommodation could not have been removed earlier.

Efforts by both the British and Irish governments after February 1996 to encourage Sinn Féin leaders to secure their place at all-party talks by persuading the IRA to renew their broken ceasefire, if not *de facto* concessions to republicans, were perceived as such by unionists. Indeed, some hardline unionists or loyalists would claim that the damaging and destructive disturbances, instigated by more aggressive and uncontrollable elements in their community in July 1996, stemmed from long pent-up frustration at such perceived partiality, and the lack of any comparable gestures to them. Moreover, many of them saw most of the arrangements agreed by the present governments for the restart of talks in September 1997, and the so-called 'confidence-building measures' undertaken since then, as directed mainly towards meeting republican requests.

Nevertheless serious – if sporadic and in the event generally counter-productive – attempts have been made to mollify unionist opinion and boost their confidence, by both the British Prime Minister, Tony Blair, and his Irish counterpart, the Taoiseach, Bertie Ahern, and these are referred to in Chapters VII and VIII. The *Hillsborough Declaration* (p. 181), issued jointly by the two leaders on 1 April 1999, was accepted by many unionists as an honest effort to allay their worries over decommissioning, and at the same time provide a means by which republicans could begin the process. After its rejection by the terrorist-linked parties, however, *The Way Forward* document, issued on 2 July (p. 183), was perceived by most unionists as reflecting the subsequent swing on the part of the two leaders to accommodate these parties and bring them back on board.

This change in emphasis confirmed for many their suspicions that the governments, having secured an agreement and peace of a sort, were so anxious to ensure that these did not break down, that they had opted to turn a blind eye to the horrific 'punishment beatings', 'kneecappings' and even killings, that still occurred. Terrorist groups supposedly on ceasefire, were widely believed to have been involved in some at least of these. Apart from the temporary exclusion from 'multi-party talks' of the UDP and Sinn Féin in early 1998, which seemed at the time to establish a moral principle and set a precedent, no action had been taken against any of the political parties linked to such groups. Pragmatism rather than principle now appeared to be the accepted standard for the British and the Irish governments – acceptance that an imperfect peace is better than no peace at all.

Given the legitimate aspirations for a united Ireland, it is not surprising that criticism of British government policy and action (or inaction) in Northern Ireland, over the years, has also come from the nationalist/republican community. Admittedly, governing a divided society is no easy matter, and in retrospect mistakes have undoubtedly been made. Nevertheless, recent British governments and those officials and bodies responsible for law and order (in very difficult circumstances and despite some inept lapses) have done as well as might reasonably have been expected of them, and in general maintained an impartial approach. For example, during the 'marching season' of 1996, in a four week period when tensions were running high, the authorities, including the police, were accused first by one side, then the other, of giving way to the greater threat of violence – an indication in itself that they were at least attempting to be even-handed. The point has to be emphasised, as this is something for which they are seldom given due credit. Again, in July 1998, when a highly sensitive Orange Order parade was restricted by the Parades Commission from proceeding along a disputed route, the police carried out their duties resolutely and quite impartially – as anyone viewing the events of that time live on television could testify. In the subsequent stand-off several of them were injured, some seriously. Before the event Sinn Féin had been very vocal and insistent in demanding that the law must be enforced; after the event republicans showed little if any appreciation for the efforts of either government or police.

Unionist Concerns

Of major concern to most unionists during the multi-party talks was the issue of the Republic's claim to the territory of Northern Ireland. Of equal concern at that time was the principle of consent, as set out and affirmed by the British and Irish governments and agreed by the SDLP – a principle that Sinn Féin never previously accepted, not even at the comparatively non-confrontational Forum for Peace and Reconciliation held in Dublin during the period of the 1994 IRA ceasefire. Both these matters have been settled to the advantage of unionists, and were written into the Good Friday Agreement. A majority of them are probably reasonably happy about these aspects of the Agreement, as they are with the establishment of a local Assembly. Such benefits are all too often overshadowed, however, by their perception that the spirit of the Agreement is not being honoured by those with terrorist links, and by their concerns regarding republican intentions.

Although some unionists consider that not only hardline republican groups, but even the moderate SDLP and the Irish government, are part of a hostile 'pan-nationalist front', most have long been prepared to negotiate and work with constitutional nationalists. However, a number, having until recently heard little (and as yet having seen virtually nothing) to convince them that republicans have indeed rejected violence for good, are still reluctant to work with Sinn Féin. They remain sceptical about that party's claims to be promoting peace – claims that have yet to be matched by tangible proof of their sincere commitment to peace *per se*, and consequently can be dismissed all too easily by the more cynical as merely part of an insidious and devious 'peace tactic'. The repeated refusal by Sinn Féin in the past to condemn any republican violence merely increased unionist suspicions. However, the statements by the party leadership since the Omagh bombing in August 1998, should not be dismissed out of hand. Nevertheless it is difficult to see how the 'huge gap of distrust' referred to by the President of Sinn Féin can effectively begin to be bridged before their words are backed up by some positive trust-building action by the IRA, with whom they are linked.

While the 1994 IRA ceasefire was announced as 'complete', the 'permanence' of that of the CLMC was to depend on there being no renewal of republican violence. The importance of words in the Northern Ireland situation has been referred to already. Thus the refusal by the IRA to confirm that their 'complete' ceasefire would be 'permanent' did nothing to allay unionist fears that they (the IRA) fully intended to resume their terror campaign, if republicans did not achieve all they wanted by democratic and non-violent means. Indeed, the semantic arguments of nationalist (SDLP) leaders, whose insistence that both words meant the same thing, merely fudged the issue and did not help solve it. When some months later the CLMC gave an assurance that loyalists would not strike first, the IRA did not respond or reciprocate. Their silence on this matter, and their failure to give some sort of reassurance without actually using the word permanent (over which they obviously had difficulty) confirmed for most unionists their worst fears about republican sincerity, and contributed to the stance adopted by many on the decommissioning of arms issue.

As it turned out, the 1994 IRA ceasefire, though arguably complete while it lasted, was certainly not permanent. Subsequent evidence that, even while officially on ceasefire, the IRA had actually been planning further violence, undoubtedly increased unionist scepticism about the credibility of any future ceasefire. Called shortly after the callous killing by the IRA of two policemen on community patrol, the renewed ceasefire, when it came, was announced as 'unequivocal'. This was the less demanding adjective required by the government on this occasion. Since then the IRA has indicated on several occasions that it will not decommission any arms at all, thus confirming cynics in their scepticism. In the months between the Agreement and the Mitchell Review, the dismissive attitude of Sinn Féin spokespersons to the issues of paramilitary weapons and continuing intimidation, kneecappings, and punishment beatings diminished (even for the most moderate of unionists) the potential significance of the more conciliatory statements of some of the party leaders during the same period. It is against this sort of background that the uncompromising attitude of many unionists to the decommissioning of weapons should be judged – however unrealistic and unreasonable their stance may appear to others. The seizure in July 1999, of weapons that were allegedly being smuggled into the country from the United States of America for IRA use, while Sinn Féin kept insisting that their ceasefire was holding, has undoubtedly deepened distrust.

The representatives of Sinn Féin, in signing up to the Mitchell Principles (p. 92) and the Declaration of Support in the Good Friday Agreement (p. 172), have renounced the use of violence for themselves, and also undertaken to oppose any use or threat of force for political purposes. Only since the Omagh massacre in August 1998, has it become clear that they are prepared to oppose, by publicly condemning, those dissident republican groups who continue to use it. However, they have not yet, as the logical follow-up to their statements since then, called specifically for the decommissioning of any 'illegally-held arms' in the possession of 'paramilitary groups' – the only weapons or groups referred to in the Agreement, which they claim to support. In the past, whenever they have been questioned about decommissioning, they have either evaded the question; indicated that they have no weapons to decommission; claimed that they are not the IRA and should not be asked to deliver; or sought to broaden the subject to include legally-held firearms and the weaponry of the security forces – aspects of decommissioning that are not even mentioned in the Agreement. Yet they have repeatedly asserted that unionists, in claiming that the decommissioning of illegally-held arms by paramilitary groups is an integral part of the Agreement, are trying to re-negotiate the document.

Republicans may consider unionist fears to be groundless, and possibly they are. However, if they want unionists to commit themselves more confidently to inclusive co-operation in the new power-sharing structures, then republican leaders, who have only recently acknowledged that decommissioning is an essential part of the peace process, need to be less ambiguous in their language and more positive in their approach. In the past, many moderate unionists have been disappointed that the SDLP, despite its undoubted opposition to violence, failed to support them in any move to secure a reduction in paramilitary violence that involved the exclusion of Sinn Féin from executive power. They have felt that the party's softly-softly approach not only let militant republicans off the hook, but possibly even re-assured them in their contemptuous disregard of the wishes of a majority in both unionist and nationalist traditions. Never-theless, the deputy leader of the SDLP, Seamus Mallon, has de-servedly earned the respect of most unionists for his straight talking. Indeed, few could have complained at his carefully con-sidered comments (reported in *The Irish News* of 29 January, 2000) that the republican movement 'cannot continue for ever … to claim the benefits of the ballot box, while at the same time denying the imperative to decommission'.

Nationalist Concerns

This section is an honest attempt to see things from a national-ist/republican perspective. Moderate nationalists as well as hardline republicans aspire to a united Ireland. The main differ-ence has essentially been one of approach and timing – of the means by which that might be achieved, and of what might be a realistic timescale. The SDLP has always rejected violence. On the other hand, Sinn Féin has implicitly condoned it – certainly prior to the Omagh bombing – by refusing to condemn unequiv-ocally all terrorist violence, irrespective of who the perpetrators or the victims might be. Regrettably, despite their more recent statements on the matter, party leaders still felt unable one year after the Agreement was signed, to publicly press the IRA to even 'see some arms put beyond use on a voluntary basis', as was suggested in the *Hillsborough Declaration*.

Apart from the question of how their common dream of a united Ireland might be achieved, both groups insist that their national aspirations and sense of identity be recognised and respected, and that the principles of parity of esteem and equal rights and opportunities for all be asserted and supported. In the past, unionists were slow to appreciate and take seriously the grievances of nationalists. As a result there still exists a perception among many on the nationalist/republican side that, in the field of politics as of parades and marches, unionists as a whole cannot really be trusted. This is a matter that unionists in general and their politicians, as well as members and supporters of the Loyal Institutions, have to address. Convincing and continuing evidence of good faith by unionists (even if they consider that they always act in good faith) could well be helpful in ensuring a just, honourable and lasting solution to the problems of the province. It is worth noting at this stage, however, as perceptive nationalists will no doubt have appreciated, that unionist insistence on the principle of consent in the current conflict implies a tacit agreement to accept possible future constitutional change, and even a united Ireland – provided such change only comes about through the freely given consent of a majority of the people of Northern Ireland.

The euphoria, raised expectations, and heightened confidence of the nationalist community as a whole, occasioned by the 1994 ceasefires and the early phase of the peace process, gradually evaporated with the subsequent slow pace of progress towards all-party talks. The apparent reluctance of the British government to initiate inclusive discussions, as well as the perceived intransigence of unionist politicians, led to deep dismay and disappointment, and to further frustration throughout the nationalist community. Then in July 1996, the hopes of moderate nationalists (and others) that the province might be on the verge of a breakthrough in favour of dialogue, were shattered by the destructive and disruptive disorder that followed the refusal of the Orange Order (supported on television news programmes by some unionist politicians) to consider any alteration to the route of a traditional parade to avoid a nationalist area. The inability of Orange Order or unionist political leaders to control disorderly camp-followers, or of the authorities to enforce the rule of law against loyalist rioters, and the bias, as nationalists inevitably saw it, of subsequent police action against them, caused not only anger and animosity among the more militant, but also deep offence and outrage, as well as resentment, among moderate and constitutional nationalists. There was a significant, if subtle, shift in the mood of moderate nationalists at that time, which could be sensed rather than defined, and which cannot be ignored or shrugged off as inconsequential. There has also been considerable concern throughout much of 1998 and 1999 at sectarian attacks on Catholics/nationalists. Most of these are probably carried out by dissident loyalist terrorist groups. However, many nationalists and republicans remain convinced that those supposedly on ceasefire have been involved in a number of the more sophisticated attacks, and that there has been police collusion in some high-profile cases.

Contentious Marches and Demonstrations
Traditional parades are very much part and parcel of the local scene in Ulster, and most but not all are associated with one or other of the Loyal Institutions. As indicated earlier, although over 90 per cent of such parades take place without any trouble, demographic changes in the last three decades have resulted in a rise in tension annually in certain strongly nationalist/ republican areas during the so-called marching season in July and August. The (Catholic/nationalist) Ancient Order of Hibernians also holds a small number of traditional parades, though only a very few pass through staunchly loyalist districts. Local residents or outside political activists seldom stir up any serious opposition or organise any significant demonstration by way of protest against these. Within the last few years, a Parades Commission, empowered to determine or restrict routes, or even prohibit parades, has been established. Unfortunately the rulings of the Commission may often disappoint and frustrate, or even provoke, one or other side, and the body itself does not receive wide support in either tradition.

Thus when tensions are running high, an orderly demonstration (even though specifically called as a peaceful protest) can be 'hijacked' by frustrated outside elements and used as cover to attack the police, who have the unenviable task of implementing the rulings of the Parades Commission and maintaining law and order. Just such an event occurred in 1998, after a traditional Orange Order parade had been refused permission to return from a service in the Church of Ireland parish church at Drumcree via the Garvaghy Road to Portadown. In this sort of tense situation, no number of local stewards can prevent the eruption elsewhere of unauthorised and unsupervised support-ive protests, with the consequent intimidation of police families, the firebombing of homes and other indefensible activity. When, many miles from the main protest, three young brothers died in a house fire started by a petrol bomb, everyone was shocked. Many who would normally support or sympathise with the Order were horrified, and an Orange Order Chaplain called for an end to the demonstration. Although such an appalling out-come was not intended or foreseen by any of the leaders of the Orange Order, who have always denied that it was the work of their members, there is little doubt that the spectacle of disorder dismayed many, and brought disgrace, dishonour and odium on the Order itself.

Local concerned residents' groups or coalitions have been formed in some Catholic areas to ensure that consent is obtained before parades can proceed through them. (The stance of repub-licans on 'consent' in this context contrasts with their prolonged opposition to the concept that 'the consent of a majority of the people of Northern Ireland' is necessary in the context of any constitutional change in the status of the province.) Some of the spokesmen of such groups have served prison sentences for ter-rorist offences, and the representatives of the Loyal Orders, con-vinced that some are more interested in provoking rather than preventing confrontation, have been reluctant to negotiate with them. Many Protestants and unionists – and others who may be neither – regard their activities as part of a province-wide cam-paign against traditional loyal institutions and culture, which

they believe has been insidiously instigated by hardline republicans, if not overtly orchestrated by them. Indeed, in August
1996, one particularly perceptive columnist in the South wrote
of a deliberate 'Wind-Up-The-Prods strategy co-ordinated by a
senior republican with a distinguished terrorist record'. Likewise, in March 1997, some significant evidence for the existence
of such a strategy was shown in a Radio Telefís Éireann television programme.

Heightened tensions in the run-up periods before the
Referendum in May and the Assembly election in June 1998,
militated against any resolution of the parades problem before it
peaked during the marching season in July. The next year, the 30
June deadline, set by the Prime Minister for agreement on the
sensitive issues of decommissioning and the formation of an
Executive, effectively stymied any chance of a late settlement on
parades before the 1999 season. Both sides have been described
by the Parades Commission as intransigent, and the chance of
agreeing a satisfactory settlement depends on the attitude of
both. It will hinge to some extent on whether the spirit of the
Good Friday Agreement is adhered to by all parties, and
whether the deal is seen to be working to the advantage of both
communities. Conversely, the future of the Agreement itself
may also depend on the resolution of the parades issue.

The Church's Peace Vocation

We, members of the Presbyterian Church in Ireland,
Called by God,
in the grace of Jesus Christ,
and the power of the Holy Spirit,
to live in faith, hope and love,
as children of our heavenly Father,
and witnesses to God's Kingdom,
publicly acknowledge our vocation to peace,
which is both the gift and mission placed on us by God.

WE BELIEVE that the same evangelical faith in Jesus Christ,
Which emboldens us to pray to God as our heavenly Father,
challenges us to develop radically new attitudes and relationships
with our neighbours in Ireland.

WE AFFIRM that to be Christian peacemakers in our own situation:
we must grasp more clearly the distinctive teaching of our Lord
which challenges the general practice of our world,
and breaks the vicious cycle of matching injury with injury,
hate with hate, ignorance with ignorance.
We must therefore be prepared to meet and talk together:
with those in our own church with whom we have disagreements;
with those from churches whose practices and beliefs differ
from our own;
with those from whom we are politically divided.

WE AFFIRM that to be Christian peacemakers in our own situation:

we must recognise the responsibility given by God to government,
and to those who serve the cause of law and order,
so as to encourage well-doing, correct evil-doers, and protect the
innocent.
We must therefore reject violence;
seek ways to advance justice and promote the welfare of the
needy;
affirm that in democratic societies all citizens are called
to share in these responsibilities;
and encourage all efforts to establish new structures of consent
and participation.

WE AFFIRM that to be Christian peacemakers in our situation:
we must be initiators of programmes of action
which will contribute to peace in our community.
We must therefore provide resources and encouragement to
enable congregations to move forward at the local level in
the field of inter-community relations.

WE UNDERSTAND peacemaking to be an affirmation
and accommodation of diversity,
and that our particular history in this land of divided communities
and recurring violence,
of mutual suspicion, fear and injury,
makes it imperative that we reassert the Church's own proper
calling
to seek peace, and the things that make for peace
in our day.

Adopted by the General Assembly, 8 June 1994

PART THREE

The Present

CHAPTER FIVE

The Peace Process and the Ceasefires

The Course of the Peace Process
The Northern Ireland Peace Process 1993-1996 – A Chronology by P. Bew and G. Gillespie is a significant and illuminating collation of official documents and statements, as well as media interviews and reports about relevant incidents and events that occurred during the period June 1993 to July 1996. In the introduction the authors suggest that the peace process, as defined by them, ended with the IRA bombing of Canary Wharf, in February, 1996. In the light of subsequent events, this brief overview carries it forward – in however fragile a form – through a series of crises, to an Agreement, a Referendum, an Assembly Election and a Review of the Agreement. (In this chapter, references to the above publication, set out as it is in chronological order, can be readily accessed by utilising the dates given, so the superscript reference numbers have been omitted from the text. If greater detail or contemporary confirmation is required in subsequent chapters, official publications such as *The Agreement,* or provincial papers such as the *Belfast Telegraph,* the *News Letter* and *The Irish News,* may be consulted.)

The Hume/Adams Discussions and the Downing Street Declaration
None of the efforts made during the 1970s and 1980s to solve the problems of the province proved successful; 'direct rule', the Sunningdale Conference, a 'power-sharing' executive and the Anglo-Irish Agreement, all failed to resolve the basic disagreements and difficulties of a divided society or bring peace any nearer. Indeed, the Anglo-Irish Agreement was arguably counter-productive. In 1993, John Hume, leader of the SDLP,

and Gerry Adams, President of Sinn Féin, began a series of meetings and eventually drew up proposals which they claimed could form the basis of agreement between the peoples of the province. On 25 September 1993, they issued a statement, indicating that they were sending a report to the Irish government for their consideration, and subsequent discussion with the British government. The full text was not made public, however – an unfortunate omission that contributed to the spread of rumour and lent support to the assertions and allegations of some in the majority community, that nationalists and republicans (together with the Irish government) constituted a pan-nationalist front. The UFF terrorist group even claimed that a murder committed on 6 October was their response to the Hume/Adams talks and the threat of this front. The Prime Minister and the Taoiseach, meeting on 29 October, outlined the necessary conditions for peace, but though applauding the efforts of the two leaders, did not go as far as to adopt their proposals.

Eventually on 15 December 1993, following a prolonged period of discussion between the British and Irish governments, the Prime Minister, John Major, and the Taoiseach, Albert Reynolds, published the Downing Street Joint Declaration. This contained several fundamental commitments and assurances to unionists and nationalists alike. Of particular significance were the following:

(i) A declaration by the Prime Minister, on behalf of the British government, confirming for everyone in the province that 'they will uphold the democratic wish of the greater number of the people of Northern Ireland on the issue of whether they prefer to support the Union or a sovereign united Ireland'; reiterating that 'they have no selfish strategic or economic interest in Northern Ireland'; and reaffirming, 'as a binding obligation', that they will introduce the necessary legislation to give effect to a united Ireland if that were agreed between the two parts of the island.

(ii) A declaration by the Taoiseach, on behalf of the Irish government, which included the principle that 'it would be wrong to attempt to impose a united Ireland, in the absence of the freely given consent of a majority of the people of Northern Ireland'. This principle was reiterated when he accepted 'on behalf of the Irish government, that the democratic right of self-determination by the people of Ireland as a whole must be achieved and exercised with and subject to the agreement and consent of a majority of the people of Northern Ireland'.

The Declaration also drew attention to 'the solemn affirmation by both governments in the Anglo-Irish Agreement that any change in the status of Northern Ireland would only come about with the consent of a majority of the people of Northern Ireland'.

The Prime Minister and the Taoiseach might reasonably have hoped that assurances in terms such as these would satisfy most on both sides – that nationalists and republicans might see that the ideal of a united Ireland could realistically be achieved by peaceful democratic means without the use or threat of terrorism, and that unionists might be reassured that no change in the constitutional status of the province would be imposed without the consent of a majority of the people of the province. Unfortunately many, republican and loyalist, nationalist and unionist alike, either did not believe the two leaders, or failed to appreciate the full significance of their Joint Declaration.

Comments in the provincial newspapers in the main reflected the views of their regular readership. Published the same evening, the *Belfast Telegraph* (read in both communities) maintained that the Declaration was balanced, but wondered if it would satisfy the extremists. The next morning the *News Letter* (read mainly by unionists) suggested that 'the Province's position as part of the United Kingdom seemed less secure', and *The Irish News* (read largely by nationalists) believed that the document was an 'attempt to create the conditions for republicans to reject violence and to enter the political process'.

The Ceasefires and the Framework Document
On 31 August 1994, the IRA announced 'a complete cessation of

military operations'. This was warmly welcomed throughout the province, with ecstatic enthusiasm in republican areas, but with some scepticism in loyalist areas. The British government noted the lack of any reference in the IRA statement to a permanent cessation, but the Irish government accepted it as implying a permanent ceasefire – which in the event it quite obviously was not. The wording of the announcement, with no subsequent 'clarification' one way or the other from the IRA, did little to reassure unionists. Announcing the end of 'operational hostilities' on 13 October 1994, the CLMC indicated that the 'permanence of our ceasefire will be ... dependent upon the continued cessation of all nationalist/republican violence'. Some ten months later, they confirmed and clarified this, stating that they would not strike first, but the IRA did not respond.

In view of early accusations of 'nit-picking' over wording and of 'clear efforts' by the British government to reduce the momentum of the peace process, and later of repeated allegations by Sinn Féin that the British government only raised the decommissioning of arms issue after the ceasefire, it is pertinent at this point to examine the actual chronology.

Regarding wording, it is evident that the word 'permanent' was being used, not only by the British but also by Irish government sources, to describe the nature of a possible future ceasefire. On 21 August 1994, the latter indicated that 'to involve Sinn Féin in political structures what is required is for Sinn Féin - IRA to call a permanent cessation of violence'. In an earlier statement in Dáil Éireann on 1 June 1994, regarding the permanence of any ceasefire, the Tánaiste and Minister for Foreign Affairs, Dick Spring, had gone even further. He had declared, 'There will have to be a verification of the handing over of arms ... there is little point in attempting to bring people into political dialogue if they are doing so on the basis of giving it a try and if it does not work returning to the bomb and the bullet. It has to be permanent and there must be evidence of it ... There can be no participation by Sinn Féin-IRA in political discussions with either government until they have made a very firm commitment that the violence has ended.'

Regarding the question of when the decommissioning of arms was first raised, the above quotation indicates that the matter was certainly being aired before the ceasefire. On the other hand, Gerry Adams, in an article in *The Irish Times*, 14 June 1995, asserted that 'the surrender of IRA weapons as a precondition to negotiations was never mentioned by the London government before August 31' – the date of the 1994 IRA 'complete cessation of military operations' announcement. He then went on to accuse the British government of acting in bad faith. However, in an earlier interview published in *The Irish News*, 8 January 1994 – nearly 8 months before that ceasefire – the Sinn Féin leader had quoted (or paraphrased) Sir Patrick Mayhew, the British Secretary of State for Northern Ireland, as having stated that 'we can discuss with Sinn Féin how the IRA can hand over their weapons'. Indeed, he emphasised the point by adding, 'I hear that reiterated again and again; by Douglas Hurd, by John Major by Patrick Mayhew.'

While none of the above would justify the (implied) deliberate use of delaying or disruptive tactics, the chronology is significant, for it confirms that, contrary to the myth widely propagated by republicans both at home and abroad, decommissioning had in fact been under discussion for some time. Indeed it was actually being promoted before the ceasefire by a high-profile, senior member of the Irish government – even if, as pointed out on a later occasion by Albert Reynolds, the Taoiseach of the time, it was not his or his government's official policy. It is, therefore, both untrue and unfair to suggest that the issue was just conjured up by British and unionist politicians after the IRA ceasefire, in order to avoid having to enter into negotiations with republicans.

On 22 February 1995, the *Framework for the Future* documents were made public; these had been drawn up by the two governments, and are usually referred to as the 'Framework Documents'. They outlined proposals as to how Northern Ireland might be governed in the future, and suggested the setting up of a new North-South body with some executive functions. In Westminster, the Prime Minister promised a 'triple lock' procedural arrangement to ensure that new proposals would not be imposed on Northern Ireland. Rather they would have to be agreed (i) by the political parties in the province, (ii) by the people of the province in a Referendum, and (iii) by Parliament, before legislation could be enacted.

The *Belfast Telegraph* observed 'there is something for everyone, of all shades of unionist or nationalist opinion, and not enough for anyone to wholeheartedly endorse'. The SDLP favoured the plan for a North-South body. Unionists generally were wary, and the UUP eventually rejected the document.

The Mitchell Report and the End of the 1994 IRA Ceasefire
On the evening of 28 November 1995, in a last minute effort to break the deadlock before the scheduled visit of the President of the United States of America, Bill Clinton, to Northern Ireland, the Taoiseach, John Bruton, and the British Prime Minister, John Major, met in London. They issued a communiqué announcing early preparatory talks, and named a three-man 'international body', to be headed by former US Senator George Mitchell, to examine and report on the decommissioning of arms issue. An escape clause was included to the effect that the report would be advisory, and that neither government was committed to accepting its recommendations in advance. The efforts of the two leaders were endorsed by President Clinton on his arrival in London the next day, en route to Northern Ireland.

The President and his wife were genuinely and warmly welcomed at all their official engagements in the province. Despite the undoubted personal success of his two day visit, the President's specific call for an end to paramilitary punishment beatings went unheeded. Although kneecappings and shootings had decreased (possibly to avoid the actual discharge of firearms during a ceasefire!) punishment beatings had increased dramatically since the start of the ceasefires – a fact confirmed in a written reply in the House of Lords on 5 December. This informed the House that 148 punishment beatings by republicans and 75 by loyalists had been carried out in the fourteen months since the IRA ceasefire, compared with a total of 45 in the fourteen months before it. Moreover, several murders of alleged drug dealers by a sinister and shadowy group, Direct Action Against Drugs, generally considered to be linked to the IRA, had occurred since the ceasefire. Meanwhile the impasse between the provincial political parties seemed set to continue.

The Mitchell Report, released on 24 January 1996, concluded that paramilitary groups would not decommission any arms before all-party talks, but suggested that some decommissioning should take place during such talks – rather than before or after them, as the opposing parties, depending on their own agenda, wanted. It further recommended that those parties involved in talks should affirm their commitment to several fundamental, democratic and non-violent principles – later to become more widely known as the Mitchell Principles. They should commit themselves to democratic and exclusively peaceful means of resolving political issues, and the total and verifiable disarmament of all paramilitary organisations; they should renounce the use of force for themselves, and oppose its use (or the threat of its use) by others; and they should agree to abide by the terms of any agreement reached.

John Major, while accepting the report, considered that unless the paramilitaries agreed to decommission weapons, a special local Election should be held in Northern Ireland to 'secure a democratic mandate for all-party negotiations'. The Irish government welcomed the report, but warned that an election would be divisive, and the SDLP agreed. There had been no political breakthrough; however, there was now a glimmer of hope that more meaningful and inclusive talks might possibly get started at last.

Then, out of the blue, the IRA ended their ceasefire on the 9 February 1996, with a massive bomb attack on Canary Wharf in London, which caused widespread damage and killed two people. Though nationalists had been growing increasingly impatient with the pace of progress, few people had been expecting such a sudden turn of events, and there was fairly general disapproval and dismay. In the months that followed, loyalist paramilitary groups, by maintaining their ceasefire, won widespread, if unexpected, approval and praise. Their own political representatives repeatedly urged them not to abandon the 'moral high ground' (relative to the IRA) by responding in kind to repeated republican provocation. Nevertheless, despite such exhortations, renewed and escalating IRA activity in Northern Ireland, including the murder of soldiers and policemen, provoked random retaliatory attacks on nationalists and republicans – however illogical, inappropriate or innocent the targets. Such attacks, even if infrequent at the time, and not specifically sanctioned by the CLMC, cast considerable doubt on the credibility of the loyalist ceasefire.

Following the breakdown of the IRA ceasefire, both governments (subsequently supported by several well-known American politicians sympathetic to the cause of Irish nationalism) insisted that the IRA should restore their broken ceasefire before Sinn Féin could enter inclusive talks. Differing views existed, however, on whether they should be allowed to take their place immediately after such a ceasefire might be called, or only after a proving period of peace. It was eventually agreed that talks should not be delayed until the IRA renewed their ceasefire, but should start whether Sinn Féin was present or not.

CHAPTER SIX

The Peace Process and the Multi-Party Talks

The Start of Multi-Party Talks
Meantime the talks about talks continued. At last the British
government, acting on the Prime Minister's earlier suggestion,
decided that the special local Election would be held in the
province at the end of May 1996. The purpose was not only to secure a democratic mandate, but also to establish a pool from
which to select negotiating teams, and to choose members for an
elected forum. The function of the selected negotiating teams
from the elected top ten political parties would be to negotiate a
political settlement. George Mitchell would chair these negotiations; all participating parties would be required to sign up to
the Mitchell Principles; and those parties linked to terrorist
groups that were not on ceasefire would be excluded from the
talks. The function of the new elected Northern Ireland Forum
would be to discuss issues relevant to promoting dialogue and
understanding in the province.

Following this Election, the UUP, DUP and UKUP, the UDP
and PUP, the SDLP and Sinn Féin, the Alliance Party, the
Woman's Coalition and the Labour Party, as the top ten political
parties, all became entitled to select teams to sit at the talks.
However, Sinn Féin was excluded because of the party's links to
the IRA, which had broken its ceasefire and was once again actively engaged in violence. The UDP and PUP were admitted, because they as political parties were prepared to abide by the
Mitchell Principles, and the paramilitary groups to which they
were linked were deemed to be on ceasefire. The talks eventually
got under way as multi-party rather than inclusive all-party
talks, on 10 June 1996.

Nationalists and republicans were never particularly interested in the concept of the local Forum. Indeed Sinn Féin always said it would not participate, and the SDLP withdrew after a short time. It is true that the Forum had no remit to discuss political or constitutional change, and was perceived by most republicans and many nationalists as just a talking-shop for unionists. Be that as it may, both parties claimed to be seeking meaningful dialogue with unionists, and to spurn any institution specifically set up to promote dialogue and understanding, however ineffectual they thought it would be in furthering their own agenda, seemed somewhat strange at best.

The Independent Review of Parades and Marches
Relations between the two main communities in the province, which had improved in the early days of the ceasefires, deteriorated significantly in July 1996, at the height of the annual marching season. Tension rose and tempers flared and there was serious rioting in loyalist areas when Orangemen were initially prevented by police from parading from Drumcree down the disputed Garvaghy Road near Portadown. When it was cleared of nationalist protesters to allow the march to proceed – as also happened some days later on the lower Ormeau Road in Belfast – serious rioting erupted in many nationalist areas. The police were accused of bias by rioters and local politicians from both communities.

On 15 July 1996, in an attempt to address this intractable and recurring problem and pre-empt future trouble, Sir Patrick Mayhew announced that an Independent Review of Parades and Marches would be set up to make recommendations for the better management of controversial parades. Faced with the task of steering a difficult course between consent and confrontation, rights and responsibilities, the members of the Review, after considering the submissions of interested parties and individuals, published their report and recommendations in January 1997. The outcome was the appointment of an independent Parades Commission which was subsequently empowered by legislation to do most of what had been recommended by the Independent Review. Both traditions have serious reservations about its role, however, and the later resignation of two high-profile Protestant/unionist members upset the balance of the Commission.

As polarisation increased, so too disagreements over the de-commissioning of arms issue continued to threaten the fragile peace process and the multi-party talks. Both the British and the Irish governments were very aware that undue delay in provid-ing Sinn Féin with sufficient assurances to enable them to rec-ommend to the IRA that they renew their ceasefire, could fur-ther antagonise republicans. They also realised that inappropriate haste and failure to establish the credibility of any such ceasefire (by disregarding unionist fears that once again it would just be a tactical move) could result in a walkout by unionist politicians from the talks.

The Renewed IRA Ceasefire
Completely new governments came to power following General Elections in May and June 1997, in both the United Kingdom and in the Republic of Ireland. The changes were seen by nation-alists in Northern Ireland, and by republicans in particular, as presenting the opportunity of a fresh approach to difficult is-sues. Most unionists were initially encouraged by a major speech by the new British Prime Minister, Tony Blair, that his 'New Labour' government which, as a result of a landslide vic-tory in the election, had a huge majority in the House of Commons, would honour the undertakings of the previous Conservative government. Dr Mo Mowlam, the newly appointed Secretary of State for Northern Ireland, was warmly welcomed when she did a walkabout in Belfast.

Shortly after her appointment, Dr Mowlam was faced with the annually recurring problem of contentious parades in the marching season. In early July widespread rioting in nationalist areas followed her decision to allow the particularly sensitive parade from Drumcree to proceed along its traditional route down the Garvaghy Road near Portadown. However, the

Orange Order cancelled or rerouted several marches before the main 12 July parades, thus averting even more serious trouble. The Secretary of State was generous in her praise of their courageous decision, as were most responsible spokespersons for the nationalist community. Some republicans, however, rubbished the move as no more than a ploy on the part of unionists and loyalists to avoid dialogue with concerned residents' groups. (Such accusations undoubtedly contributed to the stiffening of the resolve of the Loyal Institutions that they should not negotiate with republican-led residents' groups in future.)

The assurances given by both the new governments to Sinn Féin, in response to repeated calls for 'clarification', apparently convinced their leaders that the decommissioning issue would no longer be allowed to delay substantive inclusive talks. It appears that they concluded that all in all conditions were now sufficiently conducive to their cause to justify a recommendation to the IRA that they should renew their ceasefire and thus ensure the entry of Sinn Féin to these talks. 'The unequivocal restoration of the ceasefire of 1994' (described then, and referred to now, as a 'complete cessation of military operations') was duly announced by the IRA and came into effect on 20 July 1997. It was generally welcomed throughout the province, albeit with greater scepticism and without the enthusiasm or euphoria, even in republican areas, that had greeted the announcement of the 1994 ceasefire. The requirement of the two governments on this occasion was that any ceasefire should be 'unequivocal' (rather than specifically 'permanent') and this was the word the IRA used in their statement. Though unionists by and large were concerned and remained apprehensive, the British government responded by announcing that, provided the ceasefire (which the public was assured was also to apply to kneecappings and punishment beatings) was maintained in both 'word and deed' for a six-week period, Sinn Féin could enter the multi-party talks when these were reconvened in September, after the summer break.

This having been achieved, the party was officially invited to

attend the talks, and the Sinn Féin delegates formally signed up
to the Mitchell Principles on 9 September 1997. However, a few
days later an IRA spokesman pointed out that 'any consent requirement must be defined within the context of British withdrawal', and also revealed that the IRA had difficulty with the
Mitchell Principles. This was viewed by both governments with
considerable concern, and was seen by unionists as further evidence of the insincerity of republicans. It now appeared that Sinn
Féin – the party that was just about to be admitted into multi-
party talks because it had secured an unequivocal IRA ceasefire,
and the party that both governments recognised and the public
perceived as the political wing of the IRA – no longer spoke for
the IRA.

It was becoming increasingly clear that Sinn Féin, which at
one time seemed to take pride in the closeness of its relationship
with the IRA, was distancing itself on the political front from
that organisation. Their leaders would later claim that because
they were not the IRA and did not represent the IRA, they could
not be held responsible for the IRA breaking their reinstated
ceasefire, or failing to decommission any weapons.

The Reconvened Multi-party Talks
Once it became apparent that Sinn Féin would almost certainly
be admitted to talks, disagreements within unionism over how
the parties should react became more frequent and more acri-
monious. A majority of unionists probably felt that once again
they had been treated rather shabbily by the British government,
which, choosing to disregard their well-founded fears, had gone
along with the Irish government and bent over backwards to
facilitate the admission to the talks of hardline republicans.
Indeed two of the unionist parliamentary parties – the DUP and
the UKUP – had insisted from the outset that they would not negotiate with republicans so long as an implicit threat of violence
persisted. However, a significant number of unionists now felt
that, despite their well-grounded and genuine misgivings about
the sincerity of Sinn Féin and the credibility of the IRA ceasefire,

the unionist case should not go by default, and that their voice should be heard at the talks. The UUP, the largest unionist political party, while not at all happy with the government's arrangements regarding the decommissioning of arms issue in general, or the refusal of Sinn Féin to agree the principle of consent in particular, decided to consult widely over the summer months. Grass-roots constituents, as well as the leaders of industry and of the mainline churches, including the Roman Catholic Church, were consulted. The party Executive eventually endorsed the view that the UUP should be in a position to present the unionist case, and decided to give their leader, David Trimble, full support to act as he saw fit. The loyalist parties, concerned at the latest comments from the IRA regarding the Mitchell Principles, were anxious to ensure that the same stringent criteria that had been demanded of them in 1996 when they signed up to the principles, would also be applied to Sinn Féin at this stage.

The talks were scheduled to restart on 15 September 1997. While it was clear that without the DUP and the UKUP, these would be no more inclusive than when Sinn Féin had been excluded, both governments were determined to press ahead. The recent admission of that party to the talks meant that those who aspired to a united Ireland were very well represented by both moderate nationalists and hardline republicans. The problem now for both governments was to establish the credibility of the talks process by convincing the largest unionist party and the two loyalist parties that they should remain at the table.

In a last minute joint statement the two governments gave sufficient assurances on decommissioning and consent to enable David Trimble to announce that the UUP would not walk away from the talks – though he did not say whether the talks would be face-to-face around the same table, or merely 'proximity' talks under the same roof. The leaders of the loyalist parties – the PUP and the UDP – also decided to join the UUP at the talks. On the morning of 16 September, the day on which the three parties were expected to turn up at the talks' venue at Stormont, a massive car-bomb was detonated in the small town of

Markethill, Co Armagh. Although there was no loss of life, damage was extensive. The explosion itself and the timing of it were widely condemned by the two governments and most of the political parties. The spokesman for Sinn Féin, however, while regretting the bombing, went on to say, rather euphemistically, that it should be seen as an 'incentive' to get on with the process of finding a settlement – a statement that was interpreted by many as a thinly veiled threat. The IRA denied responsibility, and the Continuity IRA later admitted that it had planted the device. However, the UUP security spokesman suggested that even if it had been undertaken by such a group, it was likely to have had IRA approval, if not active support.

Both governments and a number of local politicians indicated that violence should not be allowed to disrupt progress. Apparently this was the view also of the UUP, the PUP and the UDP, for the next day their representatives all turned up at Stormont, though as expected, the DUP and the UKUP did not attend. David Trimble pointed out later, however, that he and the UUP did not intend to 'negotiate' with Sinn Féin, but to 'confront' them. This they did at the table, linking them with the IRA and the Markethill bombing, and demanding their expulsion from the talks. Their request failed, but events moved rapidly thereafter, and finally by the evening of 24 September, an agreement was reached that enabled unionists and republicans to remain at the talks. According to the rules of procedure, all participating parties were bound by the majority decision. So, though Sinn Féin voted against decommissioning and consent, all the other participating parties accepted that decommissioning of arms was an indispensable part of the negotiations, and that consent would be a guiding principle of them. Despite all the difficulties, the peace process had not collapsed completely.

In retrospect this was possibly one of the defining, if not decisive moments in the long-drawn-out and tortuous saga of the peace process. Loyalist and hardline republican political parties linked to terrorist groups, as well as moderate unionist and constitutional nationalist politicians, were actually in the same room discussing the future of the province. Admittedly some did not talk directly with those they considered to be still linked too closely to paramilitary groups, but all were in a position to put forward their own points of view, and to hear those of others. The possibly over-optimistic target suggested by the Prime Minister, of reaching a conclusion by Easter 1998, was apparently accepted by all.

The Talks Bedevilled

Despite these achievements there was no immediate or dramatic change in the tenor of the reports coming out of the multi-party talks, which seemed bedevilled at every turn by one unfortunate event after another. Moreover, tension between the two communities outside of the talks was heightened as those terrorist groups, such as the loyalist LVF and the republican INLA and Continuity IRA, that were opposed to any ceasefires or talks, continued their campaigns of violence. Furthermore, while the sincerity of the representatives and officials of both governments, who had invested much effort, energy and time in the talks, cannot be called into question, not infrequently their well intentioned endeavours were undermined by inexplicably inept and insensitive handling of predictably tricky, tense or touchy situations. One example of this was when the newly appointed Irish Minister for Foreign Affairs suggested publicly in a media interview that the proposed cross-border bodies with executive powers (favoured by nationalists and republicans, but feared by most unionists as foreshadowing a united Ireland) would be 'not unlike a government'. This inevitably reawakened resentment against Irish government interference in the affairs of the province.

At the same time, confidence in the determination of the British government to take whatever steps were necessary to protect its citizens further declined as the deficiencies of its placatory prison policies, long denounced by many as unjustifiable concessions to convicted criminals, were once again exposed at the Maze Prison. A convicted republican murderer escaped, disguised as a woman, by mingling with family visitors as they left a pre-Christmas prison party. This lapse was followed a few days after Christmas in the same prison, by the shooting dead with a smuggled firearm, of the legendary LVF leader, Billy Wright, by INLA inmates – supposedly segregated from LVF prisoners. Not surprisingly the event led to heightened tension, and even further loss of confidence in, and criticism of, a government that had failed to maintain basic standards of security in a high-security prison. The murder was of course much more than just a regrettable failure on the part of the prison authorities. The INLA would have been well aware that the killing of the high-profile leader of the LVF would inevitably provoke retaliation and revenge killings by it, and put innocent Catholics and nationalists at risk. This is precisely what happened, with a spate of murders over the New Year celebratory period and throughout most of January 1998.

Confidence in government policy was indeed at a low ebb, and this was reflected among UDA and UFF prisoners who questioned whether they should any longer support the peace process. Recognising the part paramilitary prisoners had played in persuading their comrades at large to call their ceasefires, the Secretary of State took the courageous and unprecedented step of meeting them in prison. Her gamble paid off, and she succeeded in persuading them to give the peace process a further chance.

Progress at the multi-party talks had almost ground to a halt when on 13 January 1998, the two governments issued a 'Heads of Agreement' document, which the *Belfast Telegraph* reported as having at last 'introduced some realism into the stalled discussions'. It covered cross-border relations, and Articles 2 & 3 of the Irish Constitution, and on the British side the Government of Ireland Act. Sinn Féin was unhappy with it, but the moderate nationalist SDLP, as well as the UUP, the PUP and the UDP were all prepared to discuss the document.

Meanwhile, the murders continued. Until now those political parties linked to terrorist groups had always claimed that the killings and bombings had been carried out by dissident terrorist groups that were not on ceasefire. However, when the INLA shot dead a well-known loyalist with UDA connections in his shop on the outskirts of Belfast, fears increased that paramilitary groups officially on ceasefire might also be drawn into the spiral of murders. It came as no surprise to most people, therefore, when on 22 January 1998, the Chief Constable of the Royal Ulster Constabulary (RUC) linked some of the most recent killings to the UFF. A few days later that organisation admitted that it had carried out three murders, but stated that it was renewing its ceasefire forthwith on a 'no first strike' basis.

By this time the talks venue had been moved to London for a few days special effort. Unfortunately, much of the time was taken up with the problem of how to deal with the UDP which was linked to the UFF. The admission by that group finally settled the question, but before the Secretary of State and the Irish Foreign Minister announced on 27 January that the UDP had been expelled from the talks for a period, the party representatives had already walked out. They were not readmitted until 23 February. The principle had been accepted, however, and a precedent established, that no political party could participate in the talks if a terrorist group with which it was linked was in breach of its ceasefire.

Within a fortnight of the UDP being excluded from the talks, two more murders had been committed in Belfast. On this occasion suspicion fell on the IRA, which raised the possibility that Sinn Féin might also be expelled from the talks. The party claimed that it was not the IRA, and should not be held responsible for what that group did. It warned that the whole peace process could collapse without its involvement, but the Secretary of State insisted that the integrity of the talks was paramount. By the time the Chief Constable was in a position to link the IRA to the recent murders, the talks venue had been moved for a few days to Dublin. As in London, much time was spent on considering the expulsion of a party from the talks. Unlike the UFF, the IRA made no admission of guilt, and unlike the UDP,

Sinn Féin did not voluntarily leave the table. Instead, on 17 February, the party applied to the High Court in Dublin for a judicial review of moves to have it thrown out of the negotiations. The Taoiseach, Bertie Ahern, told the Dáil that the Garda Síochána (the Irish police) believed that the IRA did have a case to answer over the recent murders. The matter had not been resolved by the time the talks process left Dublin. However, when on 20 February, the Secretary of State, as expected, announced the joint decision of the two governments to expel Sinn Féin from the talks for a short period, the legal action in the South was abandoned.

The precedent set a few weeks earlier in London had been followed, and both the British and Irish governments had made it clear that breaches of the ceasefires would not be tolerated. (Their resolve on this issue would be called into question subsequently on more than one occasion.) In the event, the exclusion period for Sinn Féin was rather less than that for the UDP. It was evident that both governments wanted the two parties to be present during the final run-up to the conclusion of the talks. However, Sinn Féin made it clear that having been expelled for a time, the party itself (and not either of the governments) would decide whether and when it would go back to the last phase of the negotiations. It could have returned to the table on 9 March, but did not do so until 23 March, having had a meeting with Tony Blair, the Prime Minister, in the interval.

Within three days of Sinn Féin's expulsion, the Continuity IRA successfully detonated two large car-bombs, which caused extensive damage in the main street of the village of Moira and in the town centre of Portadown. Subsequently other bomb devices prepared by them, or by other dissident republicans calling themselves the Real IRA, were intercepted and defused on both sides of the border. Though most of these were intended for the North, one was ready for shipment to Britain. Mortar attacks on police stations in Co Armagh caused alarm and aggravation, but no damage or injury. There were further killings by both loyalist and republican dissident groups. The LVF shot dead two young friends in the village of Poyntzpass, one a Catholic the other a Protestant, at the beginning of March. Towards the end of the month the INLA shot a retired policeman who was out shopping with his wife.

However, despite the repeated attempts by dissident terrorists from both sides to destabilise the talks, those taking part in the negotiations did not abandon their efforts to reach a settlement. On 25 March, the infinitely patient but firm chairman, George Mitchell, announced that the time for discussion was over and that it was now time for decision. He finally set a deadline for the politicians, telling them that they must come up with a settlement by midnight, 9 April 1998.

The Cliffhanging Climax to the Multi-Party Talks
Despite the deadline, and the declared determination of the political parties of both sides, and of the British and the Irish governments, that it would be met, there was no immediate evidence over the next few days either of urgency or resolve. Media reports focused rather on the continuing violence and on IRA splinter groups, on opinion polls, and on yet another government *faux pas* – this time uncovered in the content of a leaked document from the Northern Ireland Office. This led to allegations about underhand schemes being prepared by government officials to ensure the 'right result' in any Referendum that might follow a settlement. The Secretary of State, Dr Mowlam, denied that there had been any attempt to 'manipulate' anyone. She later apologised to Archbishop Robin Eames, the high-profile and respected Church of Ireland Primate, who had actually been named in the leaked paper as a churchman who might be enlisted to help influence public opinion.

By the end of March, chairman George Mitchell had indicated that he would soon table a paper outlining his best assessment of an acceptable agreement, based on his own talks with the participating parties and on a document that the Prime Minister, Tony Blair, and the Taoiseach, Bertie Ahern, were reported to be preparing. Their failure to agree the detail on schedule, however,

resulted in the Mitchell blueprint being delayed. Media speculation suggested that there was serious disagreement over the
powers to be given to cross-border structures and over the
wording of proposed changes to Articles 2 & 3 of the Irish
Constitution. The delay caused concern among unionists that
the Irish government seemed to be stalling at the last minute
over these long-awaited constitutional changes, while at the
same time insisting on full executive powers for the proposed
new cross-border bodies. There followed a spate of reports of
hastily-arranged meetings and contacts between participating
party representatives and the Taoiseach or the Prime Minister,
and between the two leaders themselves.

The draft deal document was tabled just 72 hours before the
deadline for the end of the talks. Though its contents were kept
from the public, there was no concealing the dismay and outrage it caused among unionist negotiators. They saw it as biased
in favour of nationalists and were adamant that it contained
items never discussed with them in the talks, and even accused
the Irish government of being 'too greedy'. And they were not
alone in their protests, being joined by Lord Alderdice, leader of
the cross-community Alliance Party, who commented that
unionists were not the only ones upset by the document. He not
only considered it 'disappointing', but is also quoted as having
told Tony Blair, 'if you want a deal you'd better get to Stormont
quickly'. To the Prime Minister's credit he did just that.

The Prime Minister and the Taoiseach certainly played a vital
part in the very intensive negotiations that took place over the
next three days. Both came to Belfast, Bertie Ahern doing so although his mother had just died and he had to leave for a period
to attend the funeral. Neither they nor the party representatives
had much rest or sleep. The target date came and went. There
were reports of hard bargaining, agreement just round the corner, and last minute hitches and setbacks. A prominent member
of the UUP negotiating team left the talks venue early, amid
widespread rumours of a serious disagreement in the party.
Agreement was only achieved after David Trimble, the leader of

the UUP, had asked for and received a letter of assurance on several specific issues from Tony Blair, the British Prime Minister (p. 180). What had hardly seemed possible just a few days earlier, with the talks bedevilled by one unfortunate incident after another, had actually materialised – at the end of the final late-night sitting of Good Friday, 10 April 1998. The fact that it was actually the early hours of the Saturday was probably irrelevant – the end result was hailed as historic, both on television and in most local and national newspapers.

CHAPTER SEVEN

The Peace Process and the Will of the People

The Main Points of the Agreement

The agreement reached on Good Friday, 10 April 1998, by the participants in the multi-party talks, is officially called the *Multi-Party Agreement* by both the British and Irish governments. (See p. 27 of *The Agreement* – a government publication delivered to all households in the province by early May 1998). Though referred to as the Stormont or the Belfast Agreement by some, it is popularly known as the Good Friday Agreement, or simply the Agreement. It sets out to offer an opportunity for a new beginning in relationships within Northern Ireland, within the island of Ireland and between the peoples of these islands.

The full text may be accessed in *The Agreement* mentioned above, a summary of which is included in the Appendices to Part Three. For convenience, however, the main points are mentioned very briefly below. (Although the tense used may be present or future, as in the original document, most of the structures and institutions have been established and functioned briefly before being suspended due to lack of progress on decommissioning – see Chapter Nine.)

In a *Declaration of Support* for the Agreement, the participants assert that they are 'committed to partnership, equality and mutual respect as the basis of [these] relationships'. They reaffirm their 'commitment to exclusively democratic and peaceful means of resolving differences', and their 'opposition to any use or threat of force by others for any political purpose'. They acknowledge the differences between them, but 'will endeavour to strive in every practical way towards reconciliation and rapprochement'. They accept 'that all of the institutional and constitutional arrangements ... are interlocking and interdependent'.

Moreover, in the major section entitled *Constitutional Issues* (p. 2 – *The Agreement*) 'consent' is firmly established as a fundamental principle underpinning this new beginning. The word itself is used repeatedly, and its significance enhanced by its juxtaposition with, and in the context of, other words in similar vein, such as 'wish' and 'choice', 'freely given' and 'freely exercised'. The basic 'right of self-determination' is recognised and affirmed more than once, but without arrogance and tempered by a qualifying phrase such as 'on the basis of consent'. It is acknowledged that 'it would be wrong to make any change in the status of Northern Ireland [as part of the United Kingdom] save with the consent of a majority of its people'.

It is also affirmed that 'if the people of the island of Ireland exercise their right of self-determination [on the basis of consent and agreement in both parts of the island] to bring about a united Ireland, it will be a binding obligation on both governments to introduce and support legislation in their respective parliaments to give effect to that wish.' Draft clauses and schedules for incorporation in British legislation are set out, as is Irish government draft legislation to amend Articles 2 & 3 of the Constitution of Ireland which lay claim to the territory of Northern Ireland. (The proposed legislation has since been passed.)

The Agreement deals at length and in considerable detail with many of the concerns of the two main communities in the province, along three 'strands' – within Northern Ireland, between north and south in the island of Ireland, and between the islands of Great Britain and Ireland.

Strand One provides for a democratically elected Assembly in Northern Ireland, inclusive in membership, and capable of exercising executive and legislative authority, but subject to safeguards to protect the rights and interests of all sides of the community. Appointments to a power-sharing Executive are to be made according to a specific formula (the d'Hondt system – p. 179) based on party strengths in the Assembly. Additionally, a consultative Civic Forum, comprising business, trade union and voluntary sectors, to advise on social, economic and cultural issues, will be established. (The Assembly was elected, an Executive appointed and power devolved to it. The structures noted below in Strands Two and Three were also established. The problems concerning devolution and decommissioning, and the subsequent – hopefully short-term – suspension of some of these institutions are dealt with in Chapters Eight and Nine.)

Strand Two, under a new British-Irish Agreement, provides for the setting up of a North/South Ministerial Council. It will bring together those with executive responsibilities in Northern Ireland and the Irish government, to develop consultation, co-operation and action within the island of Ireland – including co-operation through agreed implementation bodies on an all-island and cross-border basis – on matters of mutual interest within the competence of the administrations, North and South.

Strand Three, also under the new British-Irish Agreement, provides for the establishment of a British-Irish Council to promote the harmonious and mutually beneficial development of the totality of relationships among the peoples of these islands. Under the same Agreement, a British-Irish Intergovernmental Conference will be established.

Rights, safeguards and equality of opportunity are dealt with, not only as specific human rights, but also as economic, social and cultural issues. The normalisation of *security* measures consistent with the diminishing level of threat, will be periodically reviewed. (Significant measures have already been taken, but not enough or fast enough to satisfy some.)

Decommissioning of weapons is a sensitive and emotive issue, for both unionists and republicans. Although an integral part of the Agreement, it is not a specific precondition to full implementation of it – rather a moral and political obligation. No details of timing are set out in the document, which deals rather with general principles. (However, even these have been interpreted differently by the two sides – unionists concentrating on the 'spirit' of the Agreement, republicans on the letter of the document. The issue became one of the major causes of subsequent stalemate in the whole process, and may cause further problems in the future. For this reason, the section on decommissioning is quoted in full in the summary of the Agreement in the Appendices to Part Three.)

Policing is another emotive issue. An independent Commission, to enquire into and make recommendations regarding future policing arrangements, was agreed, and has already completed its work. (However, its report and Parliament's eventual decision regarding its recommendations are outside the scope of this book. Suffice it to say that some republicans, in advance of its findings, stated that the whole Agreement will fail if the RUC is not disbanded – almost a precondition that disbandment must happen.)

Prisoners convicted of terrorist offences (though the word 'terrorist' is not used in the text), are to benefit from programmes for early release – provided they are affiliated to organisations that have established and are maintaining a complete and unequivocal ceasefire. (Those parties close to republican and loyalist paramilitary groups insisted from the start of talks that prisoners should be released early. Although offensive to most others, this was agreed, and many terrorist prisoners have already been released.)

Procedures for *validation, implementation and review* are laid down. The two governments will sign a new British-Irish Agreement, which embodies understandings on constitutional issues, and replaces the 1985 Anglo-Irish Agreement. They affirm their solemn commitment to support and implement the Agreement reached by the participants in the negotiations. (For details of the new agreement, see *The Agreement* – pp. 27-30 under the main heading: *Agreement between the Government of The United Kingdom of Great Britain and Northern Ireland and the Government of Ireland*.)

Agreed Referenda have taken place in both parts of the island. Majorities of those voting in each Referendum supported the Agreement, and both governments have introduced and enacted such legislation as was necessary to give effect to it as soon as the issues of the Executive, devolution and decommissioning were agreed by the parties.

Arrangements are also in place for reviews to be carried out at any time as required. The two governments and the parties in the Assembly will in addition convene a conference four years after the Agreement comes into effect, to review and report on its operation.

The Referendum

Agreement had been reached, on paper at least, by exhausted but elated participants, in a cliffhanging climax to the protracted final stages of the multi-party talks. The quite remarkable scenes of celebration and congratulation, rather than confrontation, were seen on television screens throughout Ireland and around the world. And – amid all the emotion and euphoria surrounding the 'historic pact', and despite the media hype about the significance and symbolism of it all happening at the start of the Easter weekend – there were indeed grounds for guarded optimism and genuine hope. Never before had such a far-reaching and wide-ranging deal been struck between representatives of the two main traditions in the province, meeting specifically to address the basic problems that divided them. The question now was whether the people of the two parts of the island, both North and South, and the two communities in the North, would each approve and accept the Agreement in separate Referenda to be held on 22 May 1998.

Much of the initial emotion and euphoria, though not the more enduring hope, evaporated relatively rapidly. Moreover, there were those in both traditions who were still opposed to any compromise, and it soon became clear that a vigorous and vociferous 'No' campaign against acceptance of the Agreement in the forthcoming Referendum was already being organised. As things turned out, some of those in both communities who had worked so hard to achieve a settlement were strangely silent for a time after their initial interview comments – as if drained by their recent intensive efforts – and the 'Yes' campaign got off to a rather slow start. Nevertheless, politicians on both sides were apparently very aware that, even though an agreement had been reached, the future course of the peace process would be fraught with difficult decisions and periodic problems. There was also a general recognition that for the Agreement and the Assembly to have a realistic chance of working effectively, a majority in both communities would have to approve. A view prevalent at the time was that a 'Yes' vote of at least 70% would be required to indicate such approval.

Over the next few weeks the news in the province was dominated by arguments for and against accepting the Agreement, which were stated and restated, reworded and reworked repeatedly. It was evident relatively early in the run-up to the Referendum that old established patterns of voting would play a less predictable part in the result than in past elections. It was even suggested that the previously noted 'polarity' in the politics of the province might have been 'reversed'. Though professionals may point out that any analogy with the geological phenomenon is imprecise, and though the political scene has not changed so dramatically, some old political allegiances and alliances did indeed shift significantly, if not permanently. For these reasons the arguments and attitudes of the 'Yes' and 'No' camps in the Referendum campaign, and of the parties in the Assembly Election campaign, will be followed (in the appropriate sections) rather than the chronology of the campaigns. Likewise, as quotations from provincial newspaper reports of the time are included to reflect local reactions and perceptions, rather than to prove points, specific references have often been omitted.

There was never any real uncertainty as to how members and supporters of the moderate SDLP, the large nationalist party, would vote. However, although Sinn Féin adherents eventually (and virtually *en masse*) toed the party leadership line, initially it was by no means certain that they or a majority of republicans in general would accept the Agreement. On the other side, the mainly unionist majority community was openly and very obviously divided. Not only were the DUP and the UKUP against the Agreement, but the largest and most moderate unionist party, the UUP, was seriously split on the issue.

However, the leadership of the party, supported by both the Executive and the Council, was in favour of accepting the deal. The small loyalist parties, that is the PUP and the UDP, also endorsed it. Not surprisingly, the non-aligned parties – the Alliance Party and the Women's Coalition – were wholeheartedly in favour of the Agreement.

Reported remarks made by the various party leaders during these weeks are interesting, reflect aspects of prevailing party attitudes, and may throw some light on the arguments adopted in the debate. The SDLP leader John Hume, declared that 'to say "Yes" threatens no one' – in keeping with a non-confrontational approach that during the next eighteen months failed to secure any movement on the removal of the threat. Gerry Adams, the President of Sinn Féin, referred to 'a huge gap of distrust between nationalists and unionists'. When at a later stage, he claimed that ex-Prime Minister, John Major's 'triple-lock' safeguard had been 'reduced to a single hinge', he may have been putting his own spin on the Agreement for the benefit of party dissidents, but his remarks did little to narrow that gap. They demonstrated a lack of concern that he was further undermining unionist confidence in the peace process, by fuelling fears and reinforcing reservations about the Agreement in the minds of the undecided. When the leader of the UUP, David Trimble, said that 'we in the Ulster Unionist Party rise ... knowing that the Union is stronger than it was when we sat down', he also was trying to reassure waverers in his party and pre-empt anticipated criticism from more hardline unionists of whatever party. The leader of the DUP, the Rev Ian Paisley, deplored the 'sell-out' of the Union, and pulled no punches when pointing out the weaknesses of the Agreement. He spoke bitterly of 'an Assembly of treachery', and rallied his followers by railing almost as much against the British and Irish governments in general, and the UUP and its leader in particular, as he did against Sinn Féin/IRA. Bob McCartney, the leader of the UKUP, speaking not only as an MP but from a legal perspective as an eminent barrister, considered that the Union was 'under threat' and that 'a "Yes" vote will wipe out the Union'.

There were two distinct and completely separate 'No' campaigns – one unionist, the other hardline republican. On the unionist side, the DUP and the UKUP spearheaded a vigorous 'No' campaign against the Good Friday Agreement. Their leaders, and indeed most of their supporters, remained convinced that the renewed IRA ceasefire was not permanent, and that it did not represent a genuine renunciation of violence either by the IRA or by their political apologists in Sinn Féin. They maintained that the repeated refusal of the IRA to give up any arms underlined this point, insisted that it was the height of folly to promise places on the Executive of the new Assembly to politicians of a party whose aim was to destroy the Union, and reiterated that they would not sit in an Executive with such a party. Drawing on the considerable legal expertise of the leader of the UKUP, they argued not only that the Union with Britain would be weakened rather than strengthened by the repeal of existing British legislation under the terms of the Agreement, but that new legislation to be introduced by the British government could not unilaterally alter an agreement concluded between the British and Irish governments and several separate and independent parties. Furthermore, they denounced the failure to link the decommissioning of arms to executive responsibility, or to the early release of unrepentant and unreconstructed terrorist prisoners – loyalist or republican.

Moreover, a significant number of moderate unionists, while generally in favour of an agreement based on reasonable and reciprocal compromise, had serious reservations about these last two points. They were deeply concerned that convicted criminals, including cold-blooded murderers from paramilitary groups on both sides, would be released early from prison without serving anything approaching an appropriate or adequate sentence for their crimes. Most of them were very uneasy that decommissioning had only been mentioned in the Good Friday Agreement in very general terms rather than written into it in more specific detail. Many of them, who came to be known as 'soft nos', would normally have supported the UUP. The leaders of the 'No' campaign were confident that they could persuade a majority in the unionist community as a whole to vote 'No' in the Referendum.

Although Sinn Féin leaders and representatives had been present at the talks and had accepted the Agreement, they refused to endorse it until their Ard Fheis had given approval. There were recurring reports and rumours of dissidents defecting to Republican Sinn Féin and the Thirty-Two County Sovereignty Committee, and of moves by Sinn Féin leaders to counter or contain criticism of their involvement in any agreement. The latter group accused the leadership of censoring their members and suspending those who disagreed with them. There was talk of 'traditional republican values' and insistence that the Agreement was but a 'stepping stone' towards their objective; that long-term republican aims of an end to partition and British rule in Ireland had not changed; that the ideal of a thirty-two county socialist republic had not been attenuated or abandoned; and that the 'struggle' would continue. However, the Good Friday Agreement provided for the establishment of a provincial Assembly, and dissident groups such as Republican Sinn Féin argued vehemently that this strengthened the British presence in Ireland and made partition more permanent. The IRSP/INLA rejected the peace process, describing the Agreement as 'capitulation to reactionary unionism', and pledged to fight it. How republicans in general and Sinn Féin supporters in particular would vote, would have a significant bearing on the outcome of the forthcoming Referendum in the province, but was unpredictable at this stage.

The Sinn Féin decision regarding the response of the party to the Agreement and how the party should vote in the Referendum, had been postponed for three weeks to an Ard Fheis arranged specifically to consider this issue on 10 May 1998, in Dublin – less than two weeks from the Referendum date. At this meeting it was decided by an overwhelming majority that Sinn Féin should endorse the Good Friday Agreement, and also that the party's constitution should be amended to en-

able elected party representatives to sit in the new Northern
Ireland Assembly. (Media reports had already suggested that an
IRA convention had earlier 'cleared the way' for this change in
their 'abstentionist' policy.) Altogether, the Ard Fheis was a
major success for the Sinn Féin leadership.

Be that as it may, a great many of those in the province who
had always opposed and never condoned violence, or who had
reservations about the morality of the early release of prisoners,
were both offended and outraged by the television spectacle of
IRA terrorist prisoners (allowed out on parole specifically to attend the Ard Fheis), not only giving clenched fist salutes but
being warmly welcomed by Sinn Féin leaders and members.
Such scenes of paramilitary triumphalism and support (and
they were repeated the following week in a fairly similar situation at a loyalist UDP rally in Belfast) did nothing to encourage
those with conscientious objections and qualms about aspects of
the Agreement, to vote for it. The 'blunders' of both governments 'in setting the scene for predictable ovations', albeit as a
confidence-building measure for terrorist-linked political parties and their supporters, beggar belief. Nevertheless, following
the decisions taken at the Ard Fheis, any lingering uncertainty
about how most republicans would vote in the Referendum was
now removed.

However, how those who normally supported the UUP
would vote, remained in doubt right to the very end. An opinion
poll (conducted for the *Belfast Telegraph* and UTV by Market
Research Northern Ireland, and published on 19 May) suggested
that about 46% of them would vote 'Yes', 17% 'No', and that 35%
were still undecided. The UUP was the largest of the unionist
parties, so this uncommitted group of UUP supporters was targeted by both 'No' and 'Yes' campaigners. David Trimble, along
with most of the party leadership, urged acceptance of the deal.
They argued that although the Agreement was not perfect it was
the best that could be got, that the principle of consent was written into it, and the future of the Union was secured. The party
Executive gave its backing early to their leader, followed a week

later by the whole Council, at which 72% backed him. However, the party itself was still seriously divided on the issue. Of its sitting MPs, about half openly opposed the Agreement, and were determined to vote against it. Some were even prepared to join with the leaders of the DUP and the UKUP in opposing their own leader's line of action, or to participate in the opening of a United Unionist Office to co-ordinate the overall 'No' campaign.

Both governments were determined to do what they could to secure acceptance of the Agreement. In Northern Ireland copies of it were produced and delivered to every household in the province. Tony Blair, the British Prime Minister, realising that much would depend on how moderate unionists with genuine and valid reservations voted, made several visits to reassure them that they really had nothing to fear, and to persuade them to vote 'Yes' and accept the Agreement as a package deal. His support for it, demonstrated in his repeated visits to the province and in his speeches and pledges, was probably the single most important factor in determining how previously undecided unionists voted in the Referendum. The UUP delegation to the multi-party talks had been persuaded to accept the Agreement on the basis of a reassuring letter from the Prime Minister to their leader – a sort of 'promissory note' that was apparently interpreted by them as an undertaking that if existing provisions on decommissioning were ineffective, the British government would support changes to ensure that those connected with paramilitary organisations that were not maintaining a cease-fire, would not hold political office. So too, the statements and speeches made on his visits to the province, as well as some of the answers he gave in the House of Commons, were perceived and understood by many moderate but undecided unionists – and indeed by leading Conservatives on the opposition benches in Westminster – as confirmation that new legislation would ensure that terrorist groups adhere to the commitments made by their political apologists about using exclusively peaceful means. (Quotations from his letter to the UUP leader, his pledges to the people of the province, and one of his speeches,

are included in the Appendices to Part Three). After media reports that 'Blair lays down law on arms', a prominent UUP 'Yes'
campaign spokesman argued with some satisfaction and confidence that the Prime Minister 'has now made explicit what had
been implicit'. A senior DUP 'No' campaigner warned, however,
that 'Mr Blair's promise of legislative safeguards must be judged
against the reality that no legislation can alter the Agreement
one iota.'

In fact, in his attempt to allay fears about the lack of clarity on
certain issues in the Good Friday Agreement, Tony Blair relied
on repeating or rephrasing the fine principles and ideals embod-
ied in it, or emphasising what he apparently understood to be
the intent or the spirit of it, rather than specifying how the actual
wording of the small print of the text would bring about the intended result. The Prime Minister's powers of persuasion are
considerable, and by concentrating on the principles rather than
the detail in his pledges and reassurances, he succeeded in convincing an admittedly small but sufficient majority in the unionist community that they should vote to accept the Agreement.
(Subsequent republican insistence on a strict adherence to the
letter rather than the spirit of the Good Friday Agreement was to
lead to later disagreement and delay in its full implementation.)

Moreover, it is worth noting that during this period, as the
Prime Minister campaigned to convince undecided or 'soft no'
unionists in the North to accept the Agreement, neither national-
ist/republican politicians nor the Irish government contradicted
his assurances – at least not in a way that publicly undermined his
efforts to secure a 'Yes' vote. Nor did they seriously challenge the
interpretation being put on them by those pro-Agreement unionists who had been persuaded that British legislation would solve
the problems of decommissioning, the early release of prisoners
and the admission of Sinn Féin to the Executive, and who were
campaigning on the assumption that such an interpretation of the
Prime Minister's pledges was correct. The DUP and the UKUP,
however, and the leadership of the Conservative opposition, did
take issue with him over the fudging of such matters. Significantly,

the Secretary of State, while maintaining that decommissioning formed part of the Agreement, was always careful to point out that it was not a precondition.

Meanwhile in the Republic there was some controversy over the amendments to Articles 2 & 3 of the Constitution, though this was very low-key compared to the campaigns being fought in the North. The Taoiseach, Bertie Ahern, described the proposed amendments to the Republic's claim to Northern Ireland as 'the price of peace'. The actual question to be asked in the Referendum in the South was simply: 'Do you agree with the proposals in the 19th Amendment?' – with no specific mention of the two Articles. However, a 'Yes' vote would in effect endorse both the Agreement and the proposed amendments of Articles 2 & 3.

In overall terms, the results of the Referendum in both the North and the South were remarkable. In the Republic 94% voted 'Yes', thus accepting constitutional changes along with the Agreement. However, the turn-out was relatively low with only 56% voting. That in the North was much higher at 81%, with 71% voting 'Yes' to accept the Agreement. A naïve or uncritical assessment of these results might suggest that all the problems of the province had at last been solved and a satisfactory settlement secured! That will ultimately depend on how the implementation and the working out of the Agreement actually affects the majority in both communities. It is not possible to determine accurately how individuals voted, but anti-Agreement unionists, convinced that almost all nationalists and republicans voted for a deal tailored to their demands, reckon that a majority of unionists voted against it. Be that as it may, and whether they are right or wrong, it is fairly certain that quite a number of unionists only voted for the Agreement on the basis of the Prime Minister's pledges. However, the British and Irish governments, politicians, overseas commentators and others have tended to use the figures as a benchmark and ignore both this fact and this group, on whom the future of the Agreement might well depend, and which has become increasingly disillusioned.

The Assembly Election

The next stage in the peace process, once the Agreement had been endorsed in the Referendum, was the Election to the new Northern Ireland Assembly. There was talk of possible pacts and tactical voting, particularly as a system of proportional representation, previously employed in local elections in the province, was to be used. The familiar pattern of a deep divide between those who aspired to a united Ireland, and those who wished to maintain the Union with Britain, was likely to be complicated by a sharp split between those in favour of and those against the Agreement. Despite their defeat, the DUP and the UKUP indicated that as democrats they would not try to wreck the Assembly as many thought they would do, but would work in it 'to save the Union'. However, it appeared that they (or some of them at least) would not give lower preference votes to any who supported the Agreement – including misguided unionists who were likely to put the Union in further jeopardy. While moderate UUP supporters were unlikely to give lower order votes to hardline Sinn Féin candidates seeking election, it seemed probable that a significant number were prepared to spread these votes over candidates of other parties who were in favour of the Agreement, including moderate nationalist SDLP candidates. Sinn Féin hoped to agree some sort of a pact with the SDLP, but this would have signalled a return to the past polarity of politics, at least on the republican/nationalist side. No formal pact was concluded, however, and though it appeared that most Sinn Féin adherents were against lower order preference votes being given to any unionists – even those in favour of the Agreement – the SDLP apparently had no objections to their supporters spreading their lower order votes among other parties who were in favour of it.

The political potential of the Sinn Féin leadership's stratagem (which, according to some, involved working the Agreement, securing places on the Executive and using any opportunity 'to push the system to the limit') was not appreciated by any of the smaller dissident republican political groups. They were strongly opposed to recognising, let alone participating in, any form of government that perpetuated partition, or might give any credence to the legitimacy of British jurisdiction in any part of the island. Consequently their leaders were not interested in contesting any seats in the new provincial Assembly. Indeed their paramilitary activists continued to try to destroy the peace process by sporadic terrorist mortar attacks on police stations or by leaving car-bombs in town centres, and a polling station in a country town was destroyed the day before the Election. Thus most candidates for election to the Assembly from the nationalist/republican community were in favour of the Agreement, and many of the most bitter arguments in the Assembly Election campaign occurred between representatives of unionist/loyalist parties that were either for or against the Agreement.

Disunity in the unionist community in general and low morale among supporters of the moderate UUP in particular, was a feature of the period leading up to the Election. In addition to the continuing violence of dissident republican terrorist groups, other factors combined to exacerbate the tensions inherent in any election campaign. Some of these may appear very minor or mundane to outsiders but loomed large in the minds of many unionists who believed that their identity and culture were under threat. One difficulty for them was that there was little evidence of any change in attitude among republican supporters, even on the level of sport.

Despite the Agreement and the Referenda results in both parts of the island, and the hopes that ingrained attitudes might possibly be changing, the Gaelic Athletic Association decided not to lift its traditional ban on members of the security forces and the police participating in Gaelic games. The decision was unfortunate and unhelpful in the prevailing political climate and was perceived as sectarian. Accordingly, it was highlighted in the Assembly Election campaign by the UDP who called on the financial sponsors of the association to withhold funding from the GAA. (Regrettably similar exclusive attitudes may also adversely affect non-Gaelic sporting events, as when republican

political activists persuaded – some say pressurised – a local soc-
cer team in a republican area, whose players had voted to play a
cup fixture against an RUC team, to withdraw from the match.)

There was also a sense of unease about forthcoming marches,
reflected in newspaper headlines such as 'Deal threatened by
parades problems' and 'Parades danger looms'. Leaders of the
Orange Order had failed to change the Prime Minister's attitude
to their difficulties, and he had been unable to persuade them to
support the Agreement. Alleged government intervention had
resulted in the Parades Commission postponing the publication
of a preliminary report about future parades at a sensitive time,
a move that raised unfortunate and unsettling questions about
the independence of that body.

Sinn Féin's campaign of demonisation of the police and the
party's demands that the RUC should be disbanded, had caused
considerable concern in the unionist community. So Tony Blair's
reported and apparently unambiguous statement, given early in
the run-up to the Referendum, that 'there is no question of dis-
banding the RUC', provided some reassurance to anxious unionists that their security would not be totally abandoned. Alarm
bells sounded, however, when, as the result of another leak, it
became known that the Secretary of State, in the course of select-
ing members for the Independent Commission on Policing, had
actually consulted a Sinn Féin official (now resident in the
Republic) whom the RUC had wanted to question about an attempted murder. It seemed wholly inappropriate that the opinion of such a person (even if only one among many with widely
differing views) should have been sought in relation to the
membership of a body that would be considering the future of
policing in the province and the possible disbandment of the
RUC. Such action, however well-intentioned, did little to persuade moderate unionists with residual reservations to trust the
government and vote for pro-Agreement candidates.

In the wake of the Good Friday Agreement, the Irish government's almost indecent haste to release terrorist prisoners in the
Republic was matched by the British government's determin-

ation to introduce legislation that would provide for similar
(though not such rushed) 'accelerated releases' to be carried out
in the North – provided the terrorist organisations to which the
prisoners belonged were on ceasefire. Disappointment and disillusionment deepened as it became increasingly clear that, despite all the general assurances and pledges given by the Prime
Minister, the detail of the new legislation lacked the substance of
the safeguards many unionists, and the Conservative shadow
spokesman, had obviously thought he was promising. 'Jail release plan stands' was a fairly typical newspaper headline of
early June, 1998.

Those who had chosen the (for them) rather risky road towards a somewhat elusive peace, on the basis of perceived
promises, despite their doubts and in the face of the reproaches
and recriminations of more sceptical fellow-unionists, felt very
vulnerable and badly let down. Moreover, it appeared that apart
from a few faithful followers in the UUP leadership circle, David
Trimble was becoming more and more isolated, and his position
less and less secure – despite his enthusiasm and eloquence
about his 'vision for the future' in a speech which the DUP denounced as 'an SDLP election speech'. In fact, just a few days
before polling day, and in the face of growing apathy among
disheartened and disappointed moderate unionist supporters,
the UUP leader was warning of a possible SDLP triumph.

Newspaper headlines, reports and comments such as 'Why
your vote is vital' and 'Seize the day for the future in the most
important poll ever' exhorted everyone eligible to vote to take
the trouble to do so. Nevertheless, it was clear by the end of
polling on 25 June that the turn-out was considerably down on
that at the Referendum; this was widely interpreted as a bad
sign for the UUP. There were some nail-biting and emotional
finishes, as lower order preference votes were added to the initial first preference ones. Some party candidates, who had
worked tirelessly throughout the talks process, were pipped at
the post – the leader of the UDP narrowly failed to get elected.
By the end of the count the SDLP had won the highest number of

first preference votes. Overall, the results for the UUP were disappointing, though the party held the largest number of Assembly seats. This fact alone kept hopes alive that, despite their disillusionment, moderate unionists would not reject the Agreement.

Following the Election the final state of the parties in the Northern Ireland Assembly was as follows:

Unionist: UUP, 28; DUP, 20; UKUP, 5; PUP, 2; Others, 3.

Nationalist/Republican: SDLP, 24; Sinn Féin, 18.

Non-aligned Parties: Alliance Party, 6; Women's Coalition, 2.

To understand the significance of these results and how they might affect future progress in the Assembly, it should be noted that:

(i) The most moderate of the unionist parties was returned as the largest party, in spite of disillusionment over government failures to fulfil the Prime Minister's perceived pledges. However, there was a real possibility that some of those with serious reservations, who had remained faithful to the party, might join others who had already split off if, in the absence of any signs of movement on decommissioning, the UUP leader made too many concessions.

(ii) Although 70% of all elected Assembly members supported the Agreement, only 30 of the 57 elected unionist members did so. Since key decisions have to be taken on a cross-community basis, this did not constitute a comfortable majority.

(iii) 20 members (18 republican, 2 loyalist) represented parties with close links to terrorist organisations, and while they themselves claimed to be committed to peaceful means, they maintained that it was up to the terrorists to decide if and when they would decommission their weapons.

CHAPTER EIGHT

The Peace Process and
the Rough Road to Peace

Potholes and Pitfalls along the Path

The first meeting of the new Assembly took place within days of the election, to deal with procedural matters, and to elect a First Minister and a Deputy First Minister on a cross-community basis. (Both titles would be held as 'Designate' until such time as actual powers were devolved to the Assembly.) David Trimble, the leader of the largest party, the UUP, was nominated and elected as First Minister Designate. John Hume, leader of the second largest party, the SDLP, had indicated that he did not wish to stand, and the deputy leader of the party, Seamus Mallon, was elected as Deputy First Minister Designate. Most members were well aware that, despite the progress made and the agreement reached, major difficulties still lay ahead. Indeed serious violence, rather than peace, was a feature of the first two months following the setting up of the Assembly. This section mentions some of the events that occurred during the next nine months, to the end of March 1999. While some progress was made, there was little sign of any movement on the two main issues of decommissioning and the formation of an Executive.

In early July 1998, the long-drawn-out dispute over controversial parades erupted following the refusal by the Parades Commission to allow the proposed parade from Drumcree to march down the Garvaghy Road into Portadown. The subsequent stand-off between the RUC and the Orange Order was hijacked by unruly and undisciplined hangers-on. Mention has been made of this, and of the consequent intimidation of police families, in an earlier chapter. The deaths of three young brothers in a petrol bomb attack in another town also occurred around this time.

In late July the problem of punishment beatings and kneecappings by terrorist thugs hit the headlines again. The seriousness of kneecapping shootings lies in the potential damage that the bullet may cause to major blood vessels and nerves behind the knee – demonstrated in a most tragic way when a Catholic father of four was attacked in his home by a gang of armed men. They shot him in the knees and ripped out the telephone line. He bled to death while his partner tried to get help. The family and the police apparently had cause to believe that it was the work of the IRA. Whether it was or was not, the response of Sinn Féin representatives was both evasive and negative. Families Against Intimidation and Terror (FAIT) – a victims' support group – courageously condemned the action, and even suggested that if this was deemed to be a breach of the IRA ceasefire, then in accordance with the provisions of the Agreement, Sinn Féin should be debarred from the Executive of the Assembly.

The terrible tragedy of the Omagh bombing on Saturday, 15 August 1998, shocked the world, and the scale of it elicited the first public condemnation of republican violence by the leadership of Sinn Féin. On that day, the Real IRA – the dissident republican terrorist group that later admitted responsibility – planted a car bomb in the crowded centre of the market town of Omagh. A misleading warning about the location of the bomb was given, and shoppers and others were accordingly directed towards the bomb itself. When it exploded, 28 people were killed and over 200 were injured – with another person dying some weeks later. The victims included women and children, and Catholics, nationalists and republicans as well as Protestants and unionists. The outrage was condemned by politicians and people in both communities throughout the province, and by British and Irish politicians. Both governments have introduced 'draconian' legislation, intended to curb the activity of dissident terrorist groups. On this occasion Sinn Féin leaders, without delay or hesitation, unequivocally condemned the action. Though they have not yet overcome their difficulties in recommending that any information that might help identify republican terrorists should be handed in to the authorities, this departure by Sinn Féin from their past practice of not condemning any republican terrorist violence has been acknowledged and welcomed by unionists. The horror and revulsion generated by the Omagh bombing has been evident in both communities, and at all levels of society both North and South, and in Britain and abroad.

Prior to the second visit of Bill Clinton, President of the United States of America, to the province in early September, Gerry Adams, the President of Sinn Féin, issued a significant statement indicating that the party 'believes that the violence we have seen must be for all of us now a thing of the past, over, done with and gone'. This received a cautious welcome by the UUP leadership, as did the announcement of the appointment by Sinn Féin of a high-ranking representative to liaise with the Independent International Commission on Decommissioning (p. 177). Both reports raised hopes among pro-Agreement unionists that more tangible evidence of a new republican commitment to permanent peace might follow. The background mood for President Clinton's visit was thus set by the recent Omagh massacre, Sinn Féin's reaction to it, and the hope of the public that it might be the last atrocity of the troubles. The President's speech was headlined as a 'speech of hope'. In it he set out benchmarks for the new Northern Ireland, the first-mentioned being 'to decommission the weapons of war', and the next 'to move forward with the formation of an executive council'.

The President's visit was followed by the first one-to-one meeting between the leaders of the UUP and Sinn Féin. After it Gerry Adams commented, 'He [David Trimble] is a man I can do business with; he is a man I have to do business with; he is a man I will do business with,' while David Trimble explained, 'We are not saying you have to surrender arms or in any way feel humiliated.' Encouraging as these exchanges may have been for those who wanted the Agreement to work, there was growing concern that the suggested deadline for agreement on matters regarding cross-border co-operation and implementation bodies (the end of October) would not be met. The earlier admission by Gerry Adams that he was unable to deliver on decommissioning had been disappointing, and the lack of any evidence thereafter that the leaders of Sinn Féin were honestly or actively trying to persuade the IRA to move on the issue, merely made agreement on other matters (such as cross-border structures) more difficult. The target date passed without the hoped-for agreement.

In early December, progress toward the formation of cross-border bodies almost ground to a halt with reciprocal recriminations being bandied about by parties from both sides. The lack of progress on this front, on top of the deep-rooted disagreement on decommissioning and the establishment of an Assembly Executive, clearly frustrated both the Prime Minister and the Taoiseach. Later in the month the Nobel Peace Prize for 1998 was awarded to two of the province's leading politicians, John Hume and David Trimble, at a ceremony in Oslo. In his formal lecture the SDLP leader told of his vision for the future, while the UUP leader adopted a more pragmatic, practical and down-to-earth approach. Within days the IRA reasserted that it would not decommission any of its weapons. John Hume commented on this unhelpful and unfortunate setback in very general terms that neither criticised nor challenged anyone, while David Trimble suggested that Sinn Féin could perhaps do more to persuade the IRA to start decommissioning. For this he was accused by one of their spokespersons of trying to provoke the IRA into 'restarting the war'. He was also accused of reneging on his commitments.

Once again the UUP and the SDLP met in an attempt to negotiate a package that would allow political progress to be made before Christmas, and UUP spokesmen talked of a deal being 'tantalisingly close'. Then in the early hours of the morning, a week before Christmas, a breakthrough was announced concerning agreement on important aspects of the proposed executive departments and cross-border implementation bodies. The

same day the loyalist breakaway LVF handed in a small number
of guns and ammunition – the first gesture on decommissioning
by any terrorist organisation. The possible significance of the
move was played down by Sinn Féin who regarded it as irrelevant to the problem of IRA decommissioning, and it was also
rubbished by the PUP. The next day a senior SDLP politician
called on Sinn Féin leaders to ask the IRA to start to decommission weapons. The rather smug response did little to raise hopes
of an early resolution of the problem.

As the year drew to a close a row broke out between the
leader of the UKUP and his party's four Assembly members,
over whether the party should withdraw from the Assembly if
Sinn Féin members were appointed to the Executive before the
IRA started to decommission. A few weeks later the rebels announced the formation of yet another unionist party – the
Northern Ireland Unionist Party – the NIUP. This latest example
of disunity in the unionist camp did not affect the vital balance
between pro- and anti-Agreement unionists, however, either in
the main UUP or the Assembly as a whole.

Little changed in the first three months of 1999 during the
run-up to the first anniversary of the Good Friday Agreement.
Problems resurfaced between the UUP and the SDLP that had to
be ironed out. The UUP leader, David Trimble, came under increased pressure amid fears that two party members might vote
against the leadership line in the next Assembly vote. In the
event, just one of them deserted him, but only 50% of unionists
overall supported him, and he was left with even less room for
manoeuvre than previously. The British and Irish governments
signed a number of treaties to deal specifically with cross-border
implementation bodies, a North/South Ministerial Council, a
British-Irish Council and a British-Irish Intergovernmental
Conference – all of which were scheduled to come into effect
once an Assembly Executive was formed.

Sinn Féin and UUP leaders met to discuss their differences
but failed to resolve them. In the absence of any movement by
republicans towards the decommissioning of weapons, David

Trimble, the First Minister Designate, and his party were not prepared to sit on an Executive with Sinn Féin. In the circumstances, the Secretary of State, Dr Mowlam, had little option but to postpone the target date that had been set for the devolution of power to the Assembly, from 10 March to Good Friday, 2 April 1999 – not quite the first anniversary of the Agreement, but an emotive reminder, nevertheless, of the good intentions, the hard work, the sheer determination and the high hopes surrounding the previous Easter celebrations. She hoped that in the interval, and during their visit to America for the St Patrick's Day festivities there, the pro-Agreement party leaders might be able to reassess the issues at stake.

Meanwhile, the arguments about decommissioning and the admission of Sinn Féin to an Assembly Executive continued – the two final but critical issues that were preventing political progress at this stage. When considering the decommissioning of weapons, however, it has to be borne in mind that in addition to the IRA, the mainstream loyalist paramilitary groups (represented by the PUP and the UDP) must also decommission, and the UUP, the DUP and the UKUP have always insisted on this. However, the paramilitary-linked loyalist parties between them have only two representatives in the Assembly and no possibility of any positions on an Executive. Thus attention has been focused on Sinn Féin, with 18 Assembly members. (It is widely believed that, though the loyalist paramilitary groups on ceasefire will not get rid of arms unilaterally, they would be prepared to decommission if the IRA decided to do so. Unlike most unionist activists and voters, their political representatives do not regard decommissioning as an obligation, either moral or political. What they have been pressing for, however, is an IRA statement that 'the war is over', but even this has not been forthcoming.)

In an opinion poll – carried out by Market Solutions (NI) for the *Belfast Telegraph*, and published over three days in early February 1999 – of 1,117 respondents, 84% wanted both the IRA and loyalist paramilitaries to decommission immediately. (It should be noted that some 80% of these had previously voted

'Yes' for the Agreement, in the Referendum.) The poll indicated that 93% of Protestants and 68% of Catholics questioned, were in favour of this option. When grouped according to political preference, 97% of UUP, 91% of DUP, 70% of SDLP, 58% of Sinn Féin voters, and 85% of voters from other parties (including supporters of the PUP and the UDP), were in favour of decommissioning at that time. Sinn Féin disputed the findings and claimed that the poll was 'not worth the paper it is printed on'. However, even if allowance is made for the deficiencies of opinion polls in general, and the possibility that the figures represent an exaggerated, idealistic, and unrealistic 'wish-list' of those questioned, the findings still suggested that a significant majority from both sides really would like to see the early decommissioning of weapons. When asked if Sinn Féin should be allowed to take their seats on the Executive without IRA decommissioning, 63% of Catholics answered that they should, while 85% of Protestants replied that they should not. The poll suggested that while the stance taken by David Trimble was vindicated, his vulnerability as leader of the UUP was exposed; he would lose unionist support if he made any more concessions to republicans. The poll also indicated that an overall majority of people felt that the early release of prisoners should be halted if punishment beatings/shootings did not stop.

Findings in another poll, carried out for the BBC *Hearts & Minds* programme in March by PricewaterhouseCoopers, indicated that unionist support for the Agreement had dropped by almost 14%. Over 54% of unionists questioned had voted for it in the Referendum, but now, one year on, less than 41% of them would do so. (These figures would support suggestions made in earlier chapters concerning the significance of the Prime Minister's pre-Referendum reassurances, and subsequent unionist disenchantment.) In a question addressed to unionists only, while 43% thought the Union would be safe under the leadership of David Trimble, only 32% would continue to support him if Sinn Féin was admitted to the Executive without decommissioning – an indication of his restricted room for manoeuvre.

In the middle of February, the Taoiseach, Bertie Ahern, gave an intriguing interview to *The Sunday Times*. This caused considerable consternation and controversy among prominent Sinn Féin politicians, who immediately demanded clarification. A public relations exercise, including reassuring explanations of what he had said and meant, apparently allayed most of their concerns – the Taoiseach had not actually said that Sinn Féin should be 'barred' from the Executive, as some reports suggested. However, it appears that he did say, 'Decommissioning in one form or another has to happen. It is not compatible with being a part of a government and part of an Executive, if there is not at least a commencement to decommissioning.' Moreover, he seems to have suggested that it was 'illogical, unfair and unreasonable' that progress should be made in other areas such as prisoner releases, while nothing happens on disarmament. Two days before that interview, but overshadowed by the consequent controversy, the main editorial in *The Irish Times* made much the same point. The day after it the *Irish Independent*, another paper published in the South, declared that the Taoiseach was 'right the first time' – before the clarifications and qualified retractions! The Prime Minister, Tony Blair, apparently agreed with the Taoiseach's initial sentiments on this issue, when he used the same word 'unreasonable' in the same context, in a reply in Parliament.

Many of the province's politicians had been invited to attend the St Patrick's Day festivities in Washington, DC, but hopes that President Clinton might be able to help them overcome the last remaining obstacles to further progress – the decommissioning issue and the formation of an Assembly Executive – were not realised. The suggestion that, following on the recent comments of the Taoiseach and the Prime Minister, the President might also emphasise the desirability and the consequential benefits of early decommissioning, did not materialise. The tripartite statement issued jointly by Bill Clinton, Bertie Ahern and Tony Blair was interpreted by some as a further fudge or 'retreat' on the arms issue by the three leaders.

Meanwhile, a prominent nationalist solicitor, who had represented the Garvaghy Road Residents' Coalition, was killed
when a powerful booby trap exploded under her car as she was
leaving her home in Lurgan. The spokesman for the residents
claimed that requests for her protection had been turned down
at the highest level. Demonstrators displayed placards asserting
RUC collusion, and serious rioting occurred. There were suggestions that one of the mainstream loyalist paramilitary groups, allegedly on ceasefire, was involved, but the dissident Red Hand
Defenders later admitted that they were responsible. Religious
and political leaders from both communities condemned the
murder, which was seen as a deliberate attempt to wreck the
Agreement and the peace process.

Then, only a day before the early release, under the
Agreement, of a batch of three IRA prisoners – who though convicted in England for terrorist crimes committed there had been
transferred to Northern Ireland to complete their sentences – the
Home Secretary asked for a judicial review. He appeared to be
questioning whether early releases should be calculated in the
same way for terrorists sentenced outside the province, as for
those tried in the province. The move could hardly have been
made at a more sensitive or inappropriate time, and led to the
British government being accused not only by Sinn Féin of bad
faith, but by the DUP of double standards. The same charges
had already been levelled at the Irish government over assurances given earlier to the people of the Republic, that republican
terrorists responsible for killing a garda officer in the South,
would not get early release under the terms of the Agreement –
and their stance was also recalled at this time.

Such are the pitfalls and potholes of mutual mistrust, deliberate provocation and doctrinaire politics on both sides of the local
divide, and of unintentional but often inept and insensitive interference from officialdom in both jurisdictions, that have combined to delay and disrupt progress on the rough road to permanent peace.

One Year On

Despite all the setbacks, the British and Irish governments were anxious to resolve the stalemate. The Prime Minister and the Taoiseach both came to Hillsborough, Co Down, on the evening of 29 March 1999, and (apart from a few hours) remained through to 1 April, engaging in talks with all the pro-Agreement parties. Decommissioning and the formation of an Assembly Executive remained the major obstacles to progress. Sinn Féin insisted that the Agreement could not be re-negotiated; that decommissioning was not a precondition of appointment to the Executive, nor was it written into the Agreement; and that though they could not deliver on decommissioning, they had a right to seats on the Executive on the basis of their political support and mandate – irrespective of whether the IRA had started to decommission their weapons or not. The UUP position was that they, the other parties and the two governments had done all that was required – an Independent Commission on Policing had been set up; terrorist prisoners had been released early; cross-border bodies had been agreed; treaties had been signed; and progress had been made on all aspects of the Agreement except that of decommissioning. Republicans had to make a start on actual decommissioning.

Throughout the four days of intense discussions, spokesmen for the Taoiseach and the Prime Minister maintained an optimistic attitude, insisting that a settlement was possible by Good Friday, 2 April, though the local press was more pessimistic. In the event, after a marathon session of talks with no obvious shift in position by either side, the two leaders issued a prepared joint statement on 1 April – the *Hillsborough Declaration* – which they believed provided a way around the difficulties, and a basis for agreement. Formal discussions were adjourned until 13 April, to allow time for the local parties to study the document.

The main points suggested in the Declaration included: the nomination of Ministers to the Executive by a set date in the near future; a collective act of reconciliation, some arms 'put beyond use on a voluntary basis' in a verifiable manner, and further

moves on normalisation and demilitarisation in recognition of
the changed situation on security; the devolution of powers and
the establishment of the agreed institutions. The statement concluded with the proviso, 'It is understood by all that the successful implementation of the Agreement will be achieved if all
these steps are undertaken within the proposed time-scales; if
they are not taken, the nominations mentioned above will fall to
be confirmed by the Assembly.'

The text of the Declaration is printed in full as one of the
Appendices to Part Three. From the outset it seemed likely that
both the UUP and the SDLP would be prepared to accept the
suggestions contained in the document. In fact the nationalist
leader, John Hume, declared on television that the act of reconciliation was 'an outstanding idea'; nevertheless, there were aspects of it that apparently troubled some unionists, and the DUP
leader, the Rev Ian Paisley, called the declaration an 'April fool's
contract'.

It was fairly obvious, however, that the main objections to
the proposals contained in the declaration would come from
those parties linked to terrorist organisations that were officially
on ceasefire. The timing also was unfortunate, with the annual
commemoration of the 1916 Easter Rising just about to take
place. Sinn Féin would have difficulty in discussing, let alone
recommending at such a time, any move on disarmament that
smacked of surrender. Not surprisingly, the anniversary was
marked by hardline republican rhetoric. Gerry Adams paid tribute to the IRA and commended their volunteers of today. He
went on to say, 'One of the provocations has been the demand
on the IRA to disarm. This is something the IRA has made clear
it feels under no obligation to do.'

Over the next few days the SDLP, who backed the Declaration, challenged Sinn Féin to state that decommissioning was
an obligation. There were also indications of frustration with the
republican stance on the part of at least one junior minister in the
Irish government. While the UUP negotiating team seemed
ready to accept the document, Union First, a ginger group within

the party, set out a list of reasons why it was unacceptable. On 13 April the adjourned inter-party discussions were reconvened by the British Secretary of State and the Irish Minister for Foreign Affairs. Despite a warning by Seamus Mallon of the SDLP that Sinn Féin could not be allowed to exercise a veto on further progress after the *Hillsborough Declaration,* republicans (along with loyalists) seemed set to reject the Hillsborough proposals.

Following a meeting in London to discuss the situation with the Prime Minister, the Taoiseach admitted that they both realised that the *Hillsborough Declaration* 'has not got the widespread support we would like'. According to the *Belfast Telegraph* editorial of 16 April, the Declaration was an attempt by Mr Blair and Mr Ahern to find 'as gentle a means as they could for helping the IRA over the decommissioning hurdle'. The *Irish Times* verdict appeared on 19 April: 'Both the Dublin and London governments have accepted, reluctantly, that the *Hillsborough Declaration* will not serve as a basis for resolving the impasse over paramilitary decommissioning and the establishment of a new executive in Northern Ireland.' It described the document as 'an imaginative attempt to give both Sinn Féin and the Ulster Unionists what they say they need … Once again it seemed that the Ulster Unionists were prepared to be flexible. Sinn Féin and the IRA responded with a flat no … The "Republican family" is seemingly unable, at this time, to come to terms with its own contradictions …'

Despite the disappointment following the failure of this initiative, government sources indicated that discussions would resume at Downing Street soon. Dr Mowlam insisted that efforts to resolve the situation would continue. Seamus Mallon accused both Sinn Féin and the UUP of holding the Good Friday Agreement to ransom, and another leading spokesman for the SDLP explained that actual decommissioning had been the intention of the Agreement, but that it was not about surrender. Nevertheless, with the *Hillsborough Declaration* effectively sidelined, both the Prime Minister and the Taoiseach returned to more normal national and international business, while the local parties paused to reflect and regroup.

Interspersed and interlinked with the arguments about the root causes of the impasse that occupied much of the news in the province around this time, other local issues kept cropping up, and continued to do so. Some of these have already been considered, or at least referred to, and most are related in one way or another to the Agreement or the relationships between the two traditions. Though a few may be mentioned here and possibly later, space does not permit any detailed discussion. The issue of annual parades featured frequently in local news reports in anticipation of the marching season, and 'a long march' to highlight the civil rights of Protestants was also planned. Efforts were made by Archbishop Eames to defuse potential trouble around the parish church at Drumcree, and the Prime Minister became involved in discussions with Orangemen and residents' groups.

Punishment beatings in both communities continued, with repeated allegations that some of the terrorist groups supposedly on ceasefire were involved. The *Belfast Telegraph* reported that the police had not ruled out IRA involvement in the murder in May of a known drug-dealer who had clashed repeatedly with republicans in the past. Towards the end of June, the *Irish Independent* printed a report that 'gardaí have established that the Provisional IRA was responsible for the planned bomb attack foiled by the [recent] seizure of explosive materials'. On the other hand, dissident loyalist terrorists were reportedly responsible for most of the manifestly sectarian attacks that continued in certain areas. A woman was killed when a pipe-bomb was thrown into her home in early June. Such unacceptable goings-on fuelled a growing sense of unease and uncertainty in the three-month period before the marching season.

Toward the end of May, sombre pictures began to appear on television of gardaí at various sites in the Republic digging for the remains of people from the nationalist community who, for whatever reason, had been abducted and murdered by the IRA many years previously. That organisation had at last broken its silence of the past and agreed to give details of the sites where they had buried their victims. However, the information was often not sufficiently detailed to enable the graves to be accurately pinpointed, and the remains of only three of the nine victims named by the IRA were recovered.

Difficulties, Deadlines, and Continuing Deadlock

Following the 'sabre-rattling' at the Sinn Féin Ard Fheis early in May, and the demand by Gerry Adams that the two governments should set a new deadline to break the deadlock, suggestions appeared in the papers towards the middle of the month that the Taoiseach and the Prime Minister were about to do just that. The former was reported as saying that the parties had ten days at most to conclude a deal on the way forward. Over the next few days, there were intensive discussions in Downing Street, with confusing (and at times contradictory) reports appearing of new proposals by the two governments; of behind the scenes pressures; of journalists briefed about documents that had not been endorsed by all parties; of understandings and misunderstandings; and of agreement reached in principle that somehow came to nothing. There was a sense among many unionists, however, that having failed to move the terrorist-linked parties on their obligations, the Prime Minister and the Taoiseach had decided to bring pressure to bear on the UUP to take the required 'leap of faith' alone.

At all events, another deadline was set – with 30 June being announced as the 'absolute' or 'final' deadline. And what a deadline – with the marching season about to begin! Although the Prime Minister would show his very genuine concern by intervening personally in an attempt to solve the sensitive issue of contentious parades, he appeared blissfully unaware of the effect the potential rise in tension at the end of June might have on the latest initiative. David Trimble and the UUP negotiating team were likely to have a difficult enough time keeping increasingly uneasy pro-Agreement UUP supporters in line, without the added pressures of an imposed deadline at a predictably sensitive time.

Moreover, the main political parties had to prepare for the forthcoming Election to the European Parliament. On this occasion, the moderate UUP had to deal with internal party divisions, not only over the Agreement but also over candidate selection, as well as countering the challenge of some of the smaller unionist parties, such as the UKUP and the loyalist PUP. Moreover, the leader of the DUP, the Rev Ian Paisley, who had consistently opposed the Good Friday Agreement, had announced that, in the critical circumstances facing the province, the result should be regarded as an indicator of overall unionist opinion about the Agreement itself. He had always topped the poll in this particular Election (which was for three MEPs from Northern Ireland to sit in the European Parliament), but nationalists hoped that John Hume of the SDLP would do so on this occasion. Sinn Féin reckoned that their candidate could benefit from UUP disunity and disarray, and the splitting of the unionist vote. The turnout in the province for the Election was over 57% – well ahead of that in the rest of the UK, and possibly an indication that voters saw it as a chance to make a personal comment on the positions being adopted in the current negotiations by the various parties. In the event, the DUP leader was able to claim that once again he had come first. The SDLP leader came a good second, and the UUP candidate, despite the gloomy forecasts, managed to retain his seat. The non-aligned Alliance Party did not do particularly well.

On 15 June the Prime Minister flew into Belfast in an effort to resolve the stalemate. He used an address to Protestant and Catholic students to insist that unionists must share power with nationalists, and that republicans must accept that decommissioning can be got through but not around. His latest proposals were revealed ten days later in an article in *The Times* – apparently without advance notice to the parties. In it he described decommissioning as a 'requirement, not an option', and went on to say, 'the sequencing of whether it begins before, at or after the setting up of the executive is a matter of negotiation.' However, he saw 'merit in it happening strictly in accordance with the

Good Friday Agreement – ie. not as a prior condition – provided that (a) there was a guarantee of decommissioning by Sinn Féin; (b) it was in accordance with the timetable laid down by the Commission on Decommissioning ending with completion in May 2000; and (c) there was a cast-iron, fail-safe device that if it didn't happen according to the timetable the executive could not continue.' On this basis the UUP should accept Sinn Féin into an Executive without prior decommissioning.

The UUP leader, David Trimble, was reported as rejecting the proposed deal on the grounds that it 'was based on a promise from Sinn Féin/ IRA, which had already broken its promise over the Good Friday Agreement'. Nevertheless, Tony Blair and Bertie Ahern appeared outwardly optimistic after several hours of discussions, and announced that all the parties were committed to three principles:

(i) An inclusive Executive exercising devolved powers;

(ii) Decommissioning of all paramilitary weapons by May 2,000;

(iii) Decommissioning carried out in a manner determined by the Independent International Commission on Decommissioning (IICD).

However, when they returned to the province after the weekend, there was little sign that either Sinn Féin or the UUP were about to alter their positions before the latest deadline of 30 June. David Trimble wrote in *The Guardian* of 28 June, 'I have clearly and publicly offered to move simultaneously, that is to form an administration at the same time as decommissioning begins. This avoids any suggestion that the first move must be made by the IRA.' The *Belfast Telegraph* warmly supported this policy, headlined in its editorial as 'Jumping together'. In *The Daily Telegraph,* former Taoiseach, John Bruton highlighted the reasons why disarmament by paramilitaries was necessary, and pointed out that 'clarity, certainty and accountability' – lacking in the Agreement – were vital in regard to this issue. (A few days earlier he had suggested that his successor was adopting 'a dramatic change in strategy' by saying that the Executive should be set up in advance of decommissioning.)

There was copious coverage in the local papers of the progress of the negotiations, with the *Belfast Telegraph* using headlines such as 'The Final Countdown' and 'Moment of Truth'. On 1 July *The Irish Times* announced 'Ahern, Blair press unionists to accept SF stance', and this seems to have reflected fairly accurately the line the Prime Minister and the Taoiseach were taking. The *News Letter* declared 'Deadlock', while *The Irish News,* under the head-line 'Deadline passes', claimed that 'Sinn Féin offers an arms concession' – though it was to be 'conditional on the unionists agreeing to set up the full executive immediately'. The next day the paper reported that this offer had been rejected by the UUP, and gave further details of the Sinn Féin declaration which had been made public in a statement released by Gerry Adams late the previous evening. In it he said, 'all of us, as participants act-ing in good faith, could succeed in persuading those with arms to decommission in accordance with the agreement.'

It later transpired that when shown Sinn Féin's declaration, the UUP had suggested to them that the 'could' should be changed to a 'will' or a 'must'. In *The Irish News* of 3 July, Mr Trimble is quoted as saying, 'That was the only change we asked from them in their declaration. They went out and said we had rejected their declaration, but we only asked them to change one word. They refused to give a commitment.' That refusal finally convinced the UUP team (who were only too aware of how Sinn Féin had been sticking to the letter rather than the spirit of the Agreement) that they should not soften their 'no guns, no gov-ernment' negotiating position. Government officials hoped that General de Chastelain might be able to reassure the UUP on the issue of disarmament when he was eventually called to present the report of the IICD, but by then their decision had apparently been taken.

The Prime Minister and the Taoiseach had done what they could to persuade everyone that their suggested plan was the best that could be achieved. Tony Blair not only made a personal appeal to a meeting of all the UUP Assembly members, but also abandoned his plans to attend the opening of the new Scottish

Parliament. On 2 July 1999, the two leaders tabled their joint proposals in *The Way Forward* document – without it being endorsed by all of the pro-Agreement parties. The text is printed in full in the Appendices to Part Three. However, the main points of the plan were:

All parties to reaffirm the three principles agreed on 25 June;
The d'Hondt mechanism to nominate Ministers to be run on 15 July (p. 179);
A Devolution Order to be laid before Parliament on 15 July to take effect on 18 July;
Decommissioning to start within days as specified by General de Chastelain;
A 'fail-safe' clause to ensure that if any of these commitments are not fulfilled the governments will automatically suspend all of the institutions set up by the Agreement.

Thus ended 'a week of talk, tension and tiredness'. The Prime Minister had detected a 'seismic shift' in the attitude of Sinn Féin during the discussions, and the Taoiseach declared that 'the Rubicon has now been crossed'. Apart from *The Daily Telegraph* ('a bad day for the Union'), and the *Belfast Telegraph* ('the democrats would be penalised'), most of the papers welcomed it. Even the unionist-orientated *News Letter* suggested, 'In our view, it is eminently practicable and the politicians should take a deep breath, get in there and make it work ...' – a view probably shared by some moderate unionists. More of them were probably prepared to wait and accept David Trimble's considered assessment of the proposals. The UUP leader had little room for manoeuvre, however, in the face of increasing unease in his own party and the constant sniping of other more hardline unionists. Tony Blair (who had apparently given ground on his original proposal that only the Executive would be penalised) had assured the UUP leader that he would be shown the proposed 'fail-safe' legislation the next week. Although *The Sunday Times* editorial suggested 'Give Trimble time', the Prime Minister's article in the paper kept up the pressure by suggesting that rejection would be an 'own-goal' and the 'blame would fall on Unionists'.

Meantime, army reinforcements had arrived in the province as a massive security operation was organised in preparation for the sensitive parade from Drumcree on 4 July. However, on this occasion, even though political tensions were high, and the Orange Order had been banned from marching down the Garvaghy Road, there was not any serious trouble from hangers-on. The parade was disciplined and restrained, and after the church service a small group of local leaders marched to the police line and handed over a letter of protest before dispersing. Likewise, there was no significant trouble at the main parade on 12 July, despite marchers being banned from proceeding down the lower Ormeau Road, and the fears of nationalists that last minute rearrangements regarding route and destination might prove provocative. Dr Mo Mowlam praised the restraint shown by all sides.

The political pot was kept boiling during the week between these parades. Mr Blair's emphatic 'I can ensure that Sinn Féin aren't in the Executive if they default', not only failed to impress unionists who recalled his pre-Referendum assurances, but also angered republicans. His equally emphatic rider, 'What I can't do is ensure other parties then form a new Executive' focused attention on the SDLP. The UUP called on that party to clarify its position and stand with the democrats, but Mr Mallon claimed they were 'asking for a blank cheque'. *The Irish Times* reported on the angry reaction to the Taoiseach's remarks that Sinn Féin and the IRA were 'two separate organisations'. Though the Prime Minister later stressed they were 'effectively one movement', a leading UUP politician claimed that *The Way Forward* plan had been 'undermined to a large extent'. The *Belfast Telegraph* noted that a DUP spokesman regarded Bertie Ahern's assertion as an attempt to get Sinn Féin 'off the hook'. The paper also reported that the Taoiseach had urged the IRA to make a statement about destroying weapons.

Despite the UUP leader's insistence that *The Way Forward* proposals and the so-called fail-safe guarantee were 'unfair and flawed', on 13 July the government fast-tracked its legislation through the Commons and pushed the Northern Ireland Bill through all its stages in an eight-hour late-night sitting. This set the scene for the Secretary of State, in accordance with the above proposals, to direct the Assembly to meet and nominate members to an Executive. There were rumours that the UUP might decide not to nominate any ministers, and the Prime Minister surprised everyone by announcing that the government would amend the new legislation to meet concerns that it did not guarantee the decommissioning of terrorist weapons. However, this not only failed to satisfy the UUP, but also angered Sinn Féin, one of whose negotiators called the move 'the greatest blunder that this government has made'. Although the Taoiseach backed the British government's decision to activate the d'Hondt mechanism (p. 179) and move towards the appointment of an Assembly Executive, he was apparently taken aback and unhappy with some of the proposed amendments. The UUP Executive Council, meeting on the evening of 14 July, did not take long to effectively reject the plans of the two governments.

Nevertheless, the Assembly met as directed on the morning of 15 July, but the UUP boycotted the meeting. David Trimble announced 'I will not be making any nominations ... what should happen today is the process should not be crashed, it should be parked ...' He explained afterwards that though he wanted to move forward, he had not been given enough assurances by the government or the SDLP. Meanwhile, the d'Hondt mechanism for establishing an Executive was allowed to proceed at Stormont – a move described later by a UUP negotiator as 'clearly an exercise in political brinkmanship'. In the absence of the largest of the Assembly parties and with no unionist nominations from any other party, it was all rather unedifying – bordering even on the farcical. Those involved were aware that the new Executive, composed entirely of SDLP and Sinn Féin members, would fail to meet the cross-community requirements of the Agreement, and could not receive official authorisation. The Deputy First Minister Designate, Seamus Mallon, in a moving, dramatic and dignified personal statement, resigned his position. Of all the nationalist and republican politicians, he was probably the one most trusted by unionists in general. It was obvious he had become very frustrated by the stance of the UUP and the line of action adopted by them. The UUP may or may not have been right to reject *The Way Forward* proposals. Their boycott of the Assembly infuriated the other pro-Agreement parties, who saw it as a snub. The whole episode was regarded by many as a public relations disaster. As it was, the outcome was almost inevitable following Mr Mallon's resignation – a Review of those aspects of the Agreement that had led to the stalemate over implementation.

Provision had been made in the Agreement for 'aspects of the implementation of the multi-party agreement' to be reviewed. The Review itself was announced in the Commons by the Secretary of State on 16 July, and the Prime Minister and the Taoiseach met a few days later to set the agenda and a tight timescale. Former Senator George Mitchell, who had chaired the multi-party talks leading up to the Good Friday Agreement, agreed to act in a similar role for the Review. This was later scheduled to start on 6 September, and became known as the Mitchell Review.

When is a Ceasefire not a Ceasefire?

The IRA eventually issued its statement on 21 July, and *The Irish News* reported the next day that it 'appeared to rule out the possibility of decommissioning'. The reference in the statement to the collapse of the first 'cessation' was highlighted by the *News Letter*, which noted that the UUP saw it as 'a thinly-veiled threat'. According to the *Belfast Telegraph*, most of the other parties, apart from Sinn Féin, were also critical of the statement – the SDLP calling it 'abrupt and unhelpful', and the PUP describing it as 'an implicit threat'.

On 27 July the *Belfast Telegraph* reported that a gunrunning plot had been smashed. On 30 July it carried the story that four people – one of them linked to the IRA –had been charged with the alleged offence in the USA, and three men were being questioned in the Republic concerning the same offence. The same day it also reported that a young taxi driver, who had been missing from his home for a few days, had been found murdered. An SDLP councillor was quoted as saying 'It looks like he was interrogated and then executed by the IRA', an Alliance Party councillor suggested that Sinn Féin must distance itself from the IRA, and both the UUP and the DUP challenged Mo Mowlam to move to exclude Sinn Féin if the IRA ceasefire had been broken.

On her return in early August, Dr Mowlam decided to reassess the state of the IRA ceasefire. The murder was the fifth since the Agreement in which the IRA was allegedly implicated. Apparently there was evidence of their involvement, not only in the murders, but also in the plans to smuggle guns into the country. In a brief statement, the IRA did not deny that they had been involved in these events; they merely claimed that there was no breach of their 'cessation' and that they had not 'sanctioned' the importation of arms. Dr Mowlam's enquiry was not fully completed, however, when on 23 August, in a quite astonishing statement, made immediately after a meeting with the Secretary of State, and in her presence, the Irish Minister for Foreign Affairs, announced that 'in the round' the IRA ceasefire was intact. A few days earlier, a leading member of Sinn Féin had suggested that his party might boycott the forthcoming review of the Agreement if the IRA was penalised in any way as the result of any 'mistake' by the Secretary of State.

However, many unionists, by now thoroughly disillusioned, were convinced that the IRA ceasefire had been breached. Though not all pressed for Sinn Féin to be excluded from the forthcoming review, a majority felt that the early release of terrorist prisoners should be halted. On 26 August, Dr Mowlam announced her verdict. While apparently accepting that the evidence of involvement in the recent killing and the arms importation was 'clear', she had concluded that the IRA ceasefire had not been broken – though she admitted that she had come very close to deciding that it had. She also indicated that she had left Sinn Féin in no doubt that all violence was unacceptable.

However, Dr Mowlam made no move to stop prisoner releases, and on the basis of this verdict Sinn Féin could not be excluded from any Executive that might be formed.

While unionists in general were highly critical (the *News Letter* front page headline ran, 'An Acceptable Level Of Murder'), most politicians in the South, and nationalist leaders in the North, agreed that overall she had probably taken the wise option. *The Irish News* editorial commented, 'Few were in any doubt that the IRA was responsible ... Nationalists of all shades were disturbed by the developments and felt the credibility of the republican leadership was very much on the line ... However, ... in the most challenging of circumstances, Dr Mowlam has got it just about right.' It later quoted David Trimble, 'The challenge here for the republican movement is for them to demonstrate to the people ... that they have left violence behind.' It concluded with its own assessment, 'That deserves to be regarded in all sections of the community as an entirely reasonable and appropriate request.'

A few days later, the papers reported that the IRA had ordered several teenage boys living in republican areas to leave the country or they would be shot dead, and that a similar threat had been issued to a boy in a Protestant area by a loyalist group. These incidents were condemned by the director of the Northern Ireland Human Rights Commission, and fuelled unionist criticism of the stance of the two governments. Nevertheless, though both the UUP and Sinn Féin had indicated that they might not attend the Mitchell Review, they decided to take part, despite distrust and scepticism in both camps, and little hope in either that it would resolve their differences over decommissioning or the formation of an Executive.

Moreover, since the issue of whether the ceasefires might have been breached was raised, and following the IRA statement that its 'cessation' was intact, some media commentators have re-examined the 1994 IRA declaration of a 'complete cessation of military operations'. It has been suggested that this was so worded to cover only attacks on the security forces (both army and police), commercial targets and the Protestant/union-ist community. It apparently did not apply to those in their own community who were accused of anti-social behaviour, or those whom they judged to be informers or drug dealers. The problems of the peace process are compounded by such ambiguities of de-finition!

Following the relatively trouble-free Orange Order events at Drumcree in early July and in Belfast on the 'Twelfth', it was hoped that the Apprentice Boys' feeder parade along the lower Ormeau Road in Belfast and their main parade in Londonderry on 14 August 1999, might also pass off without serious disorder. Not only did the Apprentice Boys have a reputation of being more willing than other Loyal Orders to talk with residents' groups, but the dead and injured of the Omagh bombing were being remembered on the first anniversary of that event. However, on this occasion, the small early morning parade down the lower Ormeau Road had not been banned. The local residents' group protested and blocked the road, which the police were obliged to clear, and trouble erupted. Although the parade in Derry passed off without significant disorder, later protests turned vicious – supposedly fuelled by reports of the police action in Belfast. The *Belfast Telegraph* front page headline read, 'Jobs lost as rioting bill tops £4m mark.' The editorial com-mented that 'Petrol bomb attacks on the security forces, the torching of premises in the city centre and hijackings were clear-ly orchestrated', and went on to suggest that 'Both in the lower Ormeau and in the Bogside, serious questions must be asked of those who organised protests which brought people on to the streets.' It posed the very pertinent question, 'Do the residents' coalition groups only support the Parades Commission when it is halting marches by the loyal orders?' The issue of parades is still very much alive, and continues to influence attitudes to-ward the peace process.

So too is that of policing. The comprehensive report of the Independent Commission on Policing was released in early September. Some of the many recommendations made in it caused considerable controversy, but no decisions were taken before the New Year about which ones would be implemented. The report did not directly affect the outcome of the Mitchell Review, and must be regarded as outside the scope of this book.

On 6 September, the *Belfast Telegraph* announced the results of a poll carried out on its behalf by Market Solutions (NI) and, in its *Viewpoint* column, commented, 'When 64% of Protestants and 61% of Catholics endorse any line of action ['jumping together'] it is worth investigating, and if this includes 73% of the UUP, 71% of the SDLP, 54% of Sinn Féin and ... 51% of DUP supporters, it can be seen that a consensus is emerging.' The same paper also reported that 'Senator George Mitchell's operation to rescue the Good Friday Agreement began at Stormont today amid high hopes and low expectations.'

CHAPTER NINE

The Peace Process
and the Dawn of a New Era?

The Mitchell Review

The Mitchell Review of those aspects of the Good Friday Agreement that had led to the stalemate over implementation, lasted for over ten weeks. The relative lack of information made available by 'government sources' or party representatives to media reporters while sensitive discussions were continuing, characterised this effort to resolve the deadlock and distinguished it from previous ones. The general mood in the province was one of resignation that it was unlikely to alter the situation radically. In early October, speaking at the Conservative Party Conference, David Trimble hoped that the Review would gather pace, but indicated that he would be surprised if it ran for much longer. A Sinn Féin spokesman admitted that the political situation was not hopeful, and Gerry Adams accused the UUP of 'filibustering'. Even George Mitchell, who early in September had said he thought the Review would succeed, was warning a month later that 'the whole process is under great stress'. There followed a Cabinet reshuffle, during which Dr Mowlam, who at the time of her appointment as Secretary of State to Northern Ireland had been described as a 'breath of fresh air', was moved to London as Minister for the Cabinet Office. Peter Mandelson, who had been obliged to resign his previous post but was expected to return to high office soon, was appointed in her place.

Shortly before mid-October, Senator Mitchell, possibly hoping that more progress might be made away from the local media spotlight, not only moved the negotiations to London for a few days, but also imposed a strict news blackout. Although there were no signs of a breakthrough in the deadlock over whether an Executive could be formed before there was any movement on decommissioning, what news did emerge suggested that the atmosphere at the negotiations was better than before. Discussions between the UUP and Sinn Féin continued in Belfast while George Mitchell was in America for his young son's birthday celebrations, but the Review resumed in the more relaxed surroundings of the London venue, on his return. (There was even talk of dinner at the residence of the American ambassador, at which no mention of politics was permitted!) Gerry Adams, who had left the London talks to attend a party fundraising event in America, indicated to supporters there that he thought the Review would probably fail. Indeed, though the ambience had improved, there was still no significant political progress, and headlines such as 'Hope for Mitchell review fading' began to appear in the local papers. Within days, however, it was being suggested that Senator Mitchell apparently regarded the 'real engagement' and 'better understanding' between the UUP and Sinn Féin as progress – and so the Review continued.

Early in November George Mitchell took time out to report to the Prime Minister, the Taoiseach and President Clinton. During the next few days the focus of attention shifted temporarily to the SDLP Conference and the speeches of party leaders. In advance of the conference, the editorial of the *Belfast Telegraph* of 5 November suggested that 'the SDLP cannot escape its share of the blame for the current hiatus. Had the party been more forceful in its efforts to persuade Sinn Féin to address the weapons issue at an earlier stage, much time could have been saved.' Acknowledging that 'the SDLP played a pivotal role in the creation of the peace process ...', the paper went on to observe, 'This weekend's proceedings will provide an opportunity for the party to show that it is still centre stage, and to add its voice to those calling on the republican movement to show its commitment to democracy'. John Hume told the conference that he believed the Mitchell Review would work, and called on the party to take its rightful place at the core of the government of

Northern Ireland. Seamus Mallon suggested that none of the fears or arguments of either the UUP or Sinn Féin could justify not implementing the Agreement. Another senior SDLP negotiator was reported as saying that unionist fears of the threat of terrorist arms were no less valid or real than republican fears over surrendering arms.

On 7 November, *The Sunday Tribune* announced, 'IRA told: get ready to disarm', and went on to report that 'IRA leaders are briefing their members to expect a political deal in the North within the next two weeks.' However, as the *Belfast Telegraph* indicated the next day, 'the Ulster Unionists and Sinn Féin were both cautious today about fuelling speculation that a deal is imminent in the Mitchell Review'. The following day it reported that a Sinn Féin source had dismissed as 'totally inaccurate', speculation that the IRA might be about to decommission some of its arsenal in a tactical move. Despite such reports, on 10 November, its main headline announced a 'New IRA Formula'. A list of step by step interlocking moves – involving statements from Senator Mitchell, General de Chastelain and the IICD, the UUP, Sinn Féin and the IRA, and believed to be the outline proposals of how a deal might evolve – also appeared on the front page. The idea that a series of confidence-building statements might lead to the breaking of the deadlock over devolution and decommissioning, was developed in the media over the ensuing week.

The suggestion that David Trimble might be prepared to agree to Sinn Féin entering the Executive before the IRA decommissioned any weapons was denounced by the DUP and other anti-Agreement unionists. He was accused of abandoning his manifesto principles, breaking his promises and doing a U-turn on his party's policy of 'no guns, no government'. The UUP leader met his party's Assembly members on 11 November to inform them of the latest proposals, and recommend their acceptance. There was confusion about the outcome of the meeting – some reports suggesting that there had been 'weighty opposition' to the proposals, others that they had been rejected. It was reported that the deputy leader of the party had voted against acceptance. In the event, it appeared that a majority supported the party leader, and that the final decision would probably be taken by the full Ulster Unionist Council. Speculative press reports suggested that the final package on offer, though it did not provide either a guarantee of decommissioning, or even a statement that the war was over, would make decommissioning 'politically inevitable'. One paper mentioned an eight-week gap between the setting up of an Executive and the start of decommissioning. A *Sunday Tribune* exclusive claimed that 'IRA decommissioning would start by the end of January ... if the deal negotiated by Sinn Féin and unionists ... is accepted by the Ulster Unionist Council.'

On 16 November, *The Times* reported that Senator Mitchell 'was increasingly confident that Northern Ireland's parties could soon resolve their differences'. The *Irish News* gave a detailed account of the statement from General de Chastelain and the IICD. This included a declaration that, 'while decommissioning is an essential element of the agreement', the Commission was convinced that 'the context in which it can be achieved is the overall implementation of the agreement'; an urgent call 'on the paramilitary organisations to respond positively by appointing representatives' to hold discussions with the Commission; an explanation that 'such appointments would represent a significant confidence-building measure and would demonstrate each organisation's desire to make a further contribution to the process'; and an announcement that the Commission would now play 'a more active role'.

The same afternoon the *Belfast Telegraph* carried the full texts of statements from both Gerry Adams and David Trimble. The Sinn Féin President stated, 'Sinn Féin accepts that decommissioning is an essential part of the peace process', though he qualified this by saying that it 'can only come about on a voluntary basis'. He affirmed that the party was 'totally opposed to any use of force by others for any political purpose', and 'totally opposed to punishment attacks'. This was the first time a republican spokesperson had acknowledged the essential link between disarmament and the whole peace process.

The UUP leader insisted that 'The Ulster Unionist Party remains totally committed to the full implementation of the Belfast Agreement in all its aspects', and emphasised that the party 'is committed to the principles of inclusivity, equality and mutual respect'. He went on to say, 'If, in our view, a genuine and meaningful response is forthcoming to Monday's statement of the Independent International Commission on Decommissioning, the way will then be clear for the establishment of the political institutions envisaged in the Belfast Agreement.' His statement was greeted by renewed criticism from those unionists who had always been against the Agreement, and by some concern in his own party that he was 'taking a high risk strategy'.

The IRA issued a statement on 17 November, and the full text appeared in the papers the next day. It declared that 'The IRA is committed unequivocally to the search for freedom, justice and peace ... We acknowledge the leadership given by Sinn Féin ... The IRA is willing to further enhance the peace process and consequently, following the establishment of the institutions agreed on Good Friday last year ... will appoint a representative to enter into discussions with General John de Chastelain ...' Most unionists had probably been hoping for more clarity and certainty at this very sensitive stage, and the *Belfast Telegraph* reported that Archbishop Eames, the Church of Ireland Primate, 'admitted he was very disappointed in the language of the IRA statement'. However, he urged people to give the political process a chance, to 'think clearly, [and] allow us to see what the possibilities are'. Under the headline 'Jump with Trimble, Mitchell tells IRA', the *Belfast Telegraph* of 18 November referred to Senator Mitchell's final report, in which he concluded that 'a basis now exists for devolution to occur ... and for decommissioning to take place as soon as possible'.

Five MPs from the UUP condemned the IRA statement as 'totally inadequate', but David Trimble dissociated himself from their action. A party supporter in the Assembly commented,

'There is a possibility that we may be in business here, and business for us is achieving our party's twin objectives, decommissioning and devolution.' This was to be the UUP leadership's approach in trying to 'sell the deal' to the doubters in the party. The previous week a *Belfast Telegraph* headline had announced, 'Dump Trimble now, urges DUP leader', and predictions abounded of a serious split in the ranks of the UUP. The battle was on for the 'hearts and minds' of members prior to the Ulster Unionist Council meeting on 27 November.

The statements by Sinn Féin and the IRA were perceived by many unionists as lacking the necessary guarantees that might allow the process to proceed. UUP negotiators, however, presented them as an improvement on any previous statements issued by Sinn Féin/IRA, arguing that they must be considered together with those issued by Senator George Mitchell and General John de Chastelain. In that context they represented the best and only realistic chance of securing both the main goals of the party – devolution and decommissioning.

Their arguments were not helped, however, by two reports emerging within the week in Northern Ireland concerning the alleged comments of senior Sinn Féin members on separate visits to the USA. These suggested that once an Executive was formed, the IRA might not decommission. Both reports were disputed and dismissed as inaccurate or taken out of context. However, when news of the second incident broke, David Trimble warned that he would call off his party's decisive Council meeting if republicans tried to 'double-cross' him over arms. On 22 November, the Secretary of State suggested in the Commons that there was a default mechanism if the IRA did not decommission, and announced that he 'would not shrink from suspending the institutions if it proved necessary'. Sinn Féin insisted that there was no such mechanism in the Agreement.

'We've Jumped. You follow.'

On Saturday 27 November, more than 800 members of the Ulster Unionist Council met in the Waterfront Hall, Belfast, to decide whether to accept or reject the proposals agreed by the party negotiators at the Mitchell Review. There was considerable unease, and some speculation that support for the leader, David Trimble, was drifting away. While many agreed with his 'jump together' policy, there was talk that in the absence of any guarantee, acceptance would be 'a leap in the dark'. In the event, the motion put to the Council was as follows:

'The Ulster Unionist Council authorises the Leader and the Ulster Unionist Assembly Party to proceed as outlined in the Leader's Report and instructs the President to reconvene the Council in February 2000 to take a final decision.'

It was carried by 480 votes (58%) to 349 (42%). This was an adequate majority, though not as great as the pro-Agreement parties might have wished. In an interview after the meeting, David Trimble summed it up neatly: 'We've done our bit. Now, Mr Adams, it's over to you. We've jumped. You follow.'

The decision gave the Council opportunity to see how the situation might develop, and consider General de Chastelain's report (said to be scheduled for the end of January) regarding any material moves towards decommissioning. At the same time, it paved the way for an inclusive Executive to be formed and devolution of powers to the Assembly to proceed. It was reported that post-dated letters of resignation from the Executive would be placed with the Council by the First Minister and his party Ministers, and that they would collapse the process if the IRA reneged on the Mitchell compromise.

Sinn Féin was angered by this action, claiming it was outside the terms of the deal and was a 'precondition'. This point was reiterated in a later IRA statement, but was emphatically rejected by the UUP. The reality is that in the tense circumstances prevailing at the time, and against the background of reports about Sinn Féin loose talk overseas, the UUP leadership would probably have lost any motion of acceptance that did not contain a reliable default mechanism. Unionists saw it as a sensible 'precaution' – not a 'precondition'. (Indeed, President Clinton, when trying to persuade the UUP to agree *The Way Forward* proposals a few months earlier, had suggested the possibility of a similar course of action. He is quoted as saying, 'unionists ... can always walk away ... at a later date ...' – *The Irish Times,* 3 July.) Following the vote at the Ulster Unionist Council there were recriminations but no immediate resignations from the party. An article in *The Observer* suggested that 'the shape of unionism is changing'. Whether it is or not remains to be seen, and will to some extent be influenced by the nationalist and republican response to the UUP's 'leap of faith'.

The Assembly met on Monday 29 November to appoint a power-sharing Executive. The Secretary of State changed standing orders to allow First Ministers or Deputy First Ministers who had offered their resignation to be reappointed if the Assembly indicated that 'it wishes the member to hold the office to which he had been elected'. This was recognised by everyone as a device to ensure the return to office of Seamus Mallon as Deputy First Minister, without David Trimble having to stand for re-election as First Minister. Once Mr Mallon had been returned to post, Ministers for the agreed Departments in the Executive were nominated by their party leaders, according to the d'Hondt mechanism (p.179) and approved by the whole Assembly. The end result was that the UUP and the SDLP each secured three ministerial appointments, while the DUP and Sinn Féin each secured two. The necessary legislation for the devolution of power from Westminster to the Northern Ireland Assembly was passed in both Houses of Parliament the next day. Formal approval was granted by the Queen on Wednesday 1 December 1999, and devolution came into effect at midnight.

On Thursday 2 December 1999, the British Secretary of State for Northern Ireland, Peter Mandelson, and the Irish Minister for Foreign Affairs, David Andrews, signed the new British-Irish Agreement (p. 178) in Dublin, and shortly after that, the Taoiseach, Bertie Ahern, signed the legislation required to amend Articles 2 & 3 of the Constitution of the Republic of Ireland. At Stormont, the power-sharing Assembly Executive sat for the first time – albeit with the two DUP Ministers absent in protest at the presence of Sinn Féin in government before the

IRA decommissioned any of its weapons. The IRA announced the appointment of an interlocutor to the IICD later that evening. Within days, all the main institutions envisaged in the Good Friday Agreement had met – the North/South Council, the British-Irish Council and the British-Irish Intergovernmental Conference.

During the next few weeks the new Ministers settled into their departments, and the Executive got down to the business of running the province for real. By and large all the new power-sharing structures appeared to be working well, though there were a few teething problems for some Ministers. However, most people in the province seemed prepared to make allowances during the honeymoon period. Moreover, in the first week of the new millennium the IRA issued a statement indicating that their representative had met General de Chastelain and that further discussions would take place. While this was interpreted by some as progress, the statement reiterated the republican view that the UUP had imposed new conditions for political progress by unilaterally setting a deadline for the handover of weapons, and criticised both the RUC and British intelligence for the 'continuation of the war against republicans'.

False Dawn?
On 13 January 2000, *The Irish Times* reported that the Taoiseach, Bertie Ahern, had appealed to the republican movement to recognise that 'old arguments about surrender are no longer relevant' – particularly as it had two senior members inside the 'cabinet'. An opinion poll conducted on behalf of the same paper by MRBI Ltd., and published the next week, showed that 86% of voters in the South supported decommissioning of paramilitary weapons now. On 27 January, *The Irish News* commented that 'the vast majority of nationalists want to see the decommissioning issue resolved immediately', and predicted that 'northern nationalists ... would be appalled if any failure in this area resulted in the collapse of the Executive.'

It was becoming clear that there was unlikely to be any de-

commissioning by the end of the month, when General de
Chastelain was expected to deliver the progress report of the
IICD. It was already evident that the UUP leadership would not
be in a position to sustain the new structures of the Agreement
unless the IRA had started to decommission by that date. They
have always insisted that they had made this clear to those involved in the Mitchell Review and that it was understood by all,
though Sinn Féin have disputed this. It was widely believed that
if there was not a start to decommissioning, the reconvened
Ulster Unionist Council (due to meet on 12 February) would no
longer support David Trimble, and that he and the UUP
Ministers on the Executive would resign, possibly even before
the meeting. As a result, the Executive and much else besides
would collapse – unless the Secretary of State suspended the
Executive. Suspension, it was claimed, would be a less disas-
trous option, as the structures might possibly be reactivated.
Peter Mandelson had already indicated that, however reluctantly, he would be prepared to take such action if any party failed
to meet its obligations on devolution or decommissioning.
Republicans, who equated suspension with collapse, insisted
that this would be a mistake, and that it would make decommissioning more difficult. Nationalists also felt that the institutions
should not be suspended, though most of them apparently
agreed with their deputy leader, Seamus Mallon, that there was
now 'no excuse, no reason' for the IRA not to decommission.

The report from General de Chastelain and the IICD was received by the two governments late on 31 January. However, it
was decided not to publish it immediately, which led to speculation that relatively little progress had been made on the arms
issue. There followed a flurry of political activity in London,
Dublin and Belfast. The Secretary of State made a statement in
the Commons on the evening of 3 February. He acknowledged
that the engagement of the main paramilitary groups with the
de Chastelain Commission 'is a significant advance', and noted
that 'the Commission's report points to a number of other positive factors. He referred to the ceasefires, the silence of the guns

and 'the assurance, repeated this week, that there is no threat to the peace process from the IRA'. However, he pointed out that 'the report also stated that there has not yet been any decommissioning of arms by any major paramilitary group.' He indicated that the Commission needed further evidence to substantiate their earlier conclusion, in December, that decommissioning would occur – 'they need definite information about when decommissioning will actually start.'

The Secretary of State suggested that the institutions can only work on the basis of cross-community confidence, and without clarity over decommissioning this would quickly ebb. 'All parties must have certainty that all aspects of the Good Friday Agreement are being implemented without some being forgotten and others overlooked. If it becomes clear that because of a loss of confidence the institutions cannot be sustained, the government has to be ready to put on hold those institutions.' He went on to explain that it was 'our purpose ... to preserve them from collapse and to create the time and space in which to rebuild the confidence required to sustain them. 'I shall, therefore, publish a Bill tomorrow to enable us to institute such a pause, should one become necessary, despite our best efforts.' This would suspend the Executive, the North-South Ministerial Council and the British-Irish Council, and reactivate direct rule. The legislation would be debated the following week, and all the stages and formalities should be completed by 11 February. However, if in the interval General de Chastelain and his Commission reported that the IRA had made further and sufficient progress, the suspension would be reconsidered.

In the subsequent exchanges in the House of Commons, David Trimble maintained that 'the basis on which we proceeded to devolution has been falsified. We cannot continue in the administration with those who have disappointed the hopes we created.' Seamus Mallon pleaded passionately that the institutions should not be suspended. He suggested that the IRA should be asked: 'One: Will you decommission? Two: If yes, when will you decommission?' Media reports indicated that the

Taoiseach was concerned that no precipitate action should be taken, and that evening he flew to meet the Prime Minister (on tour in the West Country) and update him on progress. Regarding decommissioning, Tony Blair declared, 'That issue has to be confronted and resolved ... in a clear way'. 'For the Irish government's part,' Bertie Ahern explained, 'this issue has to be confronted once and for all. We must have clarity.' For the next few days 'clarity' was to be the new watchword. Seamus Mallon, of the SDLP, writing at the weekend in *The Sunday Tribune* concluded: 'What we need is clarity, what we need is certainty, what we need is commencement – if we have these, suspension need not and should not happen.' Most UUP politicians would probably have approved these points.

Pressure continued to mount for the IRA to make the move that could ensure that the power-sharing Executive continued to function. *The Irish Times* editorial of 4 February spoke of 'swift and substantial movement from the IRA'. *The Irish News* editorial the next day read, 'The onus is on republicans.' For once, most American newspapers were highly critical of the republican movement. Nevertheless, their leaders continued to insist that decommissioning could only come about when those who had weapons were convinced that politics was working. One spokesman claimed that the British government had been 'spooked' by unionists; another that 'suspension would be the greatest disaster to befall Ireland in the last 100 years'. Gerry Adams took Peter Mandelson to task for having accused the IRA of 'betraying' the peace process, and the IRA, in a statement issued on 5 February, rejected any such allegations. The statement, which reiterated that the peace process was under no threat from the IRA but warned that decommissioning will not occur on British or unionist terms, was widely reported in the Sunday papers. *The Sunday Times* described as most significant the paragraph in which the IRA recognised that 'the issue of arms needs to be dealt with in an acceptable way', while *The Sunday Tribune* noted that it was the first time the organisation had acknowledged this.

On the evening of Sunday, 6 February, the dissident Continuity IRA which was not on ceasefire, detonated a bomb at an hotel in Irvinestown, Co Fermanagh. Most commentators agreed that the purpose was to further pressurise the mainstream IRA at a very difficult time. Republican leaders condemned the action, while unionists saw it as a powerful reason for the government not to reduce or withdraw army patrols at this stage. Writing in *The Irish News* of 7 February, John Hume suggested 'that if the IRA were to arrange with General de Chastelain that an amount of Semtex was to be left in a certain location, the current difficulties could be swiftly overcome'. He appealed to them to show their 'deep respect for the will of the Irish people', and 'to demonstrate for all to see their patriotism ... through beginning voluntarily the process of decommissioning'. In the past he had usually been careful not to antagonise republicans, but this time his unusually forthright and specific statement angered Sinn Féin, who described it as unhelpful. The next day the Bill to reverse devolution was passed in the Commons. The Sinn Féin leader indicated that if the Executive was suspended, he and his party would have to reconsider whether they should participate in any review process.

Dr Seamus Hegarty, the Roman Catholic Bishop of Derry, writing in *The Irish News* of 9 February, offered 'to act as guarantor and supervisor for the safekeeping of a quantity of weapons of war, on the clear understanding that, under the auspices of General de Chastelain, they will be put beyond use'. The next day *The Irish News* carried two pertinent headlines – on the front page: 'SF cautious on bishop's move', and on the politics page: 'Bishop's arms offer lauded'. *The Irish Times* noted that 'a variety of sources' said his idea 'would not form part of any package recommended by the two governments'. The *Belfast Telegraph* reported on the concern of the Sinn Féin leadership that the party was being made a 'scapegoat' for the present crisis over decommissioning, and on their demand for 'immediate moves by the government on demilitarisation'. By now the Bill to reverse devolution had passed through all its stages in both the Commons and the Lords, and the Queen had given her assent. The decision to trigger it rested with the Secretary of State.

Intense discussions took place throughout the day, much of the night and the next day. *The Irish Times* of 11 February reminded readers of 'what the Taoiseach, Mr Ahern, made clear some days ago. What is required of the IRA now is not immediate 'product' [the UUP term], but clarity and certainty of intention'. There was, however, little clarity or certainty in the reports that reached the public at large, other than that the Secretary of State announced late in the afternoon of 11 February that he had suspended the institutions. He emphasised that his action was undertaken to save the institutions from the chaos of collapse that would have followed the resignation of Mr Trimble, or his rejection by the Ulster Unionist Council the next day.

The various versions of the sequence of events were both conflicting and confusing. According to one, Peter Mandelson had let all concerned know that he would make his decision by late afternoon. He was not informed of details of the 'major breakthrough' that Sinn Féin and the IRA were working on, until after the decision had been made, and he did not see the text of General de Chastelain's second report until after he had announced that he had, with regret, suspended the Assembly institutions. However, Sinn Féin insisted that they had kept the Secretary of State informed that significant progress was being made. According to *The Irish News*, Gerry Adams claimed that Mr Mandelson 'had collapsed the institutions in the knowledge there had been a major breakthrough'. David Trimble, however, said that he had been given no significant details of any such breakthrough at a meeting that afternoon with a Sinn Féin Minister, or in a subsequent telephone conversation with Gerry Adams. It was suggested that the breakthrough offer was conditional on David Trimble withdrawing his letter of resignation and postponing the meeting of the Ulster Unionist Council, and on the Secretary of State rescinding the suspension legislation.

The two latest reports of the de Chastelain Commission were published around this time, the second within a few hours of the first. The details in the report dated 31 January did not differ from those conveyed by the Secretary of State to MPs in the Commons on 3 February. The report confirmed that there had been 'further discussions with representatives of the IRA, the UVF and UFF'. The IRA contact had assured the Commission of 'unequivocal support ... for the peace process' and 'emphasised that there is no threat to the peace process from the IRA'. The report continued: ' All of these factors are significant. But our sole task is decommissioning and to date we have received no inform- ation from the IRA as to when decommissioning will start.' It also indicated that the loyalist paramilitary groups were pre- pared to consider decommissioning. The UVF will not do so, however, 'until it has received an unequivocal statement from the IRA that the war is over', and the UFF will not 'until it is clear that the IRA will also decommission'. It concluded: 'If it be- comes clear that decommissioning is not to happen, the Com- mission will recommend ... that it be disbanded.'

The report of General de Chastelain and the IICD dated 11 February is printed in full in the Appendices to Part Three. It certainly gave a more optimistic assessment. It indicated 'the real prospect of an agreement which would enable the Commission to fulfil the substance of its mandate'. However, the 'particularly significant ... assertion ... that the IRA will consider how to put arms and explosives beyond use in the context of the full imple- mentation of the Good Friday Agreement, and in the context of the removal of the causes of the conflict', lacked clarity and cer- tainty – the very ingredients called for by both the deputy leader of the SDLP and the Irish government the previous week. Indeed, as one commentator said, it raised more questions than it answered.

Nevertheless, the Sinn Féin view that Peter Mandelson had made a serious mistake was apparently supported by the SDLP deputy leader, Seamus Mallon. Furthermore, it was suggested that the Irish government would have preferred that suspension be postponed, in the hope that David Trimble could eventually be persuaded that sufficient progress on decommissioning had been made, and would somehow manage to convince the Ulster Unionist Council of the merits of further delay. As a result of the suspension, however, pressure was removed from the UUP leader who emerged from the Council meeting on 12 February, with his authority, if anything, strengthened.

Whatever the truth of the matter, or the rights or wrongs of the decisions made, or who might have been to blame, there is no doubt that the unionist community as a whole, including many moderate unionists, felt badly let down – particularly as they had taken the leap of faith that the other pro-Agreement parties and the two governments had urged them to take. There is little doubt that their confidence had largely evaporated, and had the Secretary of State not suspended the institutions, the UUP would have felt they had no option but to collapse them. None of those who openly criticised the handling of the situation by the Secretary of State made any suggestion as to how this aspect of the difficulty could have been dealt with.

To balance these broadly unionist views, some opinions culled from non-unionist daily papers, are included below. *The Irish News* editorial commented: 'Many of the circumstances surrounding the suspension of the executive and the meeting of the Ulster Unionist Council 24 hours later were unsatisfactory. Republicans produced a proposal of considerable significance on Friday, but regrettably did not release it publicly until an unfeasibly late stage in the proceedings ... It should have been put forward immediately after the Omagh bombing eighteen months ago ... Even if the scheme had emerged during the Mitchell review in November last, a radically different and much more positive scenario would have evolved. Some senior republicans claim that whatever proposals they put forward last week would have been rejected by unionists. In fact the blueprint contained in the second report from General de Chastelain fell short of what was requested by Seamus Mallon ... However, the plan can still form a firm basis for the next and decisive review of the agreement. The hints yesterday from Mr Mallon that the authorities are in possession of further crucial details about the intentions of the IRA deserve to be clarified swiftly.'

The *Irish Independent* of 14 February noted, 'There should be no more fudging on this issue [of arms]. As Seamus Mallon has rightly said, we need to know if the IRA intends to decommission. And if so, when. How is a matter for General de Chastelain's commission.' *The Irish Times* carried headlines such as, 'Mallon criticises "faulty decision"', and 'British capitulated to pressure from UUP, says Adams'. The secondary heading of the Taoiseach's article in the same paper read, 'The de Chastelain commission now believes for the first time that it has a commitment from the IRA that decommissioning will indeed happen. That is a huge advance, says the Taoiseach, Bertie Ahern, and we must move quickly.'

In this article the Taoiseach wrote, 'I can confirm ... the deep significance of the last two paragraphs [6 & 7] of the de Chastelain report.' Paragraph 5, however, is central to the whole report, and for unionists the ambiguities of 'context', with connotations of possible political 'preconditions', certainly require 'clarification' – all words that have featured frequently in recent republican rhetoric. Mr Ahern went on to acknowledge that, 'It is, of course natural that people should wish to have reassurance about what is involved ... I believe it is right that David Trimble should seek such assurance from General de Chastelain ... I am sure the leadership of Sinn Féin will also wish to be helpful.'

Sadly, however, republican leaders declined to give any clarification on the interpretation of 'context', insisting that unionists should accept the report as it stood. Lack of clarity and certainty may not be 'the root causes of conflict' referred to by the IRA, but they have without doubt contributed to past failures to resolve them, and both governments and all parties should seek to avoid fudge in any future negotiations. Moreover, when so much significant progress had apparently been made by both political and militant republicans in such a short time, when under pressure (so it is said) from the Irish government, it is most disheartening that the fundamental issue of arms had not been seriously faced up to earlier.

On 16 February, the day before the Prime Minister and the Taoiseach were due to meet in an effort to resolve the suspension issue, the IRA put out a statement, announcing an end to their engagement with the IICD, and withdrawing all the propositions put to the Commission since November. This is a serious setback, though hopefully not the end of the peace process. If the content of their withdrawn offer were made public and proved to be as significant as those backing it believe it to be, it could possibly form the basis for further discussion and more lasting agreement in the not too distant future.

This book has been five years in the writing. It had been hoped to end it on a high note – but the Agreement, the Referendum and the establishment of a provincial Assembly, the Hillsborough Declaration one year on, and most recently the Mitchell Review, have all been followed by further difficulties and disappointment. So it is ending at a low point with the suspension of the power-sharing Executive and other institutions, and the withdrawal of the IRA from contact with the Commission set up to oversee the arms issue. Nevertheless, there are possibly more signs of hope for the future than there were five years ago.

Although polarisation always occurs at times of tension, and people are tempted to think that the other tradition will never change, there have been significant shifts on both sides – if not as rapid or as radical as individual people or parties might have wished. Sinn Féin members of the republican movement have actually sat in a 'partitionist' Assembly. Moderate unionists of the UUP have actually shared power with nationalists and republicans in an Executive. Aspirations may not and need not change. Attitudes may and should, and there is evidence that they are changing – just consider the consensus in the post-Agreement opinion polls about decommissioning. Hope is still alive in and for Northern Ireland.

EPILOGUE

Hanging on to Hope

Peace is possible in Northern Ireland, and most of the people of the province continue to hope that the present 'imperfect' or 'armed' peace may become a permanent peace. That the province has moved as far as it has on the path towards such a peace is in no small measure due to those national leaders and others, who in their time as Prime Minister, Taoiseach, Secretary of State or other role, have not despaired of the problems of the past, or accepted that these were insurmountable. Despite disappointments and delays, misunderstandings and mistakes, they have hung on to their belief in the people and to the hope of a better future. They have inevitably attracted a fair amount of adverse comment and criticism from time to time and from both sides of the community, and some of this has been referred to earlier. They are all due their fair share of credit, however, for their patience and persistence. So too are those, unfamiliar with the politics or the traditions of Northern Ireland, who have helped steer the parties through the twists and turns of protracted talks and a lengthy Review. Local leaders, who have had the courage to break out of the pattern of past politics, also deserve recognition and two have already been honoured on the international stage. It has been said that 'without John Hume there would have been no peace process, and without David Trimble there would have been no Agreement.' Although they may differ in their approach, most local politicians are sensitive to the hopes and aspirations of those they represent, yet endeavour in their own way to promote the welfare of the whole community.

Credit must also be given to the ordinary people of the province, who have had to put up with frustration and fear, anxiety and grief, insecurity and uncertainty about the future. Although both traditions do sincerely desire peace, there is still much misunderstanding and downright distrust of the other community, and of their intentions, and these have got to be addressed.

Today, as a result of the ceasefires of the opposing paramilitary groups, though still without any promise of permanent peace, many in the province are enjoying a prolonged period of relative peace. Yet even this appreciation of a less-than-perfect peace overlooks the fact that the so-called peace process has not yet removed fear or brought peace to everyone. Fascist elements in extremist groups still seek to control community behaviour from time to time. Callous, cold-blooded kneecappings and horrific, inhuman punishment beatings (that should be totally unacceptable in a civilised or Christian society) still occur sporadically in certain areas and in both communities. Despite the claims of the IRA that 'the guns are silent', and of mainstream loyalist paramilitaries that they have not been involved in killings or other sectarian attacks, the gun has not yet been removed from politics, and the threat of violence remains.

President Mary McAleese, on the occasion of receiving an honorary degree at the Queen's University of Belfast in December 1998, is reported as saying, 'Out of ... the chaos of a culture of conflict ... we now have a chance to build a new culture of consensus ...' Both traditions in the province take legitimate pride in and demand respect for their culture. President McAleese's concept of a new culture does not impinge on or diminish either; rather it complements both. It may be developed further by examining the source and origin of the word itself. According to the *Chambers 21st Century Dictionary*, 'culture' (from Latin *cultura*) derives ultimately from *colere*; so too does the related word 'cultivate' (from Latin *cultivare*). The meaning of *colere* can cover: to cherish or to practise, to till or to take care of. The idea that this 'new culture' must be 'cultivated' – with the suggestion of ongoing effort, of patient but persistent nurturing and tending to ensure growth and prevent withering – is possibly helpful at this time.

The Agreement (the first tender shoot of the new culture) was eventually provided with a supporting stake in the shape of the actual implementation of agreed structures. However, it is as likely to wither and die from the lack of watering or warmth in the form of decommissioning, as it was from the delay in the setting up of the inclusive Executive and cross-border bodies – frustrating though that delay may have been to some. Indeed, it may even yet fail to survive, without the stimulus of a start to decommissioning and the support of the restoration of devolution and the agreed institutions.

Inflexible and intransigent attitudes, contentious and confrontational approaches, old and outdated mindsets that harp back to past conflicts, perceived injustices or unfulfilled dreams, present-day tendencies to demand rights and ignore responsibilities, all contribute to the current problems of the province, and can and should be actively addressed by both communities. The full implementation of all aspects of the Agreement is an important factor in reversing these problems, and unionist politicians have now honoured their commitments under that Agreement. Decommissioning is also an essential part of the whole peace process, and this has been acknowledged by republican political leaders – albeit not yet put into practice by their more militant activists.

Admittedly there is much more to establishing trust and building confidence than the single issue of decommissioning. However, without it being seriously addressed once and for all, and decommissioning being achieved in an acceptable manner, the people of the province cannot fully emerge from 'the old culture of conflict', or freely enjoy 'the new culture of consensus'. Meanwhile, the silent majority continue to hope and pray for real peace and genuine reconciliation in the near future.

APPENDIX I

A Summary of the Multi-Party Agreement

Popularly known as the Good Friday Agreement, or simply the Agreement, the agreement reached on Good Friday, 10 April 1998, by the participants in the multi-party talks, is also referred to by some as the Stormont Agreement, and by others as the Belfast Agreement. It is officially called the Multi-Party Agreement by both the British and Irish Governments in the text of the Agreement between the Government of the United Kingdom of Great Britain and Northern Ireland and the Government of Ireland – a separate but closely related and parallel agreement between the two governments, but not the other participants in the talks. (See p. 27 of *The Agreement* – a Government publication delivered to all households in the province by early May 1998. Throughout this summary, free and frequent use is made of phrases and whole sentences from *The Agreement;* where whole paragraphs or sections are quoted in full, this is stated.)

The Agreement is prefaced by a *Declaration of Support* in which the participants in the multi-party talks declare that they are committed to partnership, equality and mutual respect as the basis for relationships within Northern Ireland, between North and South, and between these islands. They reaffirm their total and absolute commitment to exclusively peaceful means of resolving differences and their opposition to any use or threat of force by others for any political purposes. They acknowledge the differences between their political aspirations, but pledge that they will, in good faith, work to ensure the success of each and every one of the arrangements to be established under the agreement.

It is accepted 'that all of the institutional and constitutional arrangements – an Assembly in Northern Ireland, a North/South Ministerial Council, implementation bodies, a British-Irish Council and a British-Irish Intergovernmental Conference, and amendments to British Acts of Parliament and the Constitution of Ireland – are interlocking and interdependent and that in particular the functioning of the Assembly and the North/South Council are so closely inter-related that the success of each depends on that of the other.'

In the first main section entitled *Constitutional Issues* (which because of the importance to both traditions in the province of the fundamental principles set out in it, is printed in full below) the participants endorse the commitment made by both the British and Irish Governments, that in a new British-Irish Agreement replacing the Anglo-Irish Agreement, they will:

'(i) recognise the legitimacy of whatever choice is freely exercised by a majority of the people of Northern Ireland with regard to its status, whether they prefer to continue to support the Union with Great Britain or a sovereign united Ireland;

(ii) recognise that it is for the people of the island of Ireland alone, by agreement between the two parts respectively and without external impediment, to exercise their right of self-determination on the basis of consent, freely and concurrently given, North and South, to bring about a united Ireland, if that is their wish, accepting that this right must be achieved and exercised with and subject to the agreement and consent of a majority of the people of Northern Ireland;

(iii) acknowledge that while a substantial section of the people in Northern Ireland share the legitimate wish of a majority of the people of the island of Ireland for a united Ireland, the present wish of a majority of the people of Northern Ireland, freely exercised and legitimate, is to maintain the Union and, accordingly, that Northern Ireland's status as part of the United Kingdom reflects and relies upon that wish; and that it would be wrong to make any change in the status of Northern Ireland save with the consent of a majority of its people;

(iv) affirm that if, in the future, the people of the island of Ireland exercise their right of self-determination on the basis set out in sections (i) and (ii) above to bring about a united Ireland, it will be binding on both Governments to introduce and support in their respective Parliaments legislation to give effect to that wish;

(v) affirm that whatever choice is freely exercised by a majority of the people of Northern Ireland, the power of the sovereign government with jurisdiction there shall be exercised with rigorous impartiality on behalf of all the people in the diversity of their identities and traditions and shall be founded on the principles of full respect for, and equality of, civil, political, social and cultural rights, of freedom from discrimination for all citizens, and parity of esteem and of just and equal treatment for the identity, ethos, and aspirations of both communities;

(vi) recognise the birthright of all the people of Northern Ireland to identify themselves and be accepted as Irish or British, or both, as they may so choose, and accordingly confirm that their right to hold both British and Irish citizenship is accepted by both Governments and would not be affected by any future change in the status of Northern Ireland.'

The participants also note that the two Governments have accordingly undertaken in the context of this comprehensive political agreement to propose and support changes in the Constitution of Ireland and in British legislation relating to the constitutional status of Northern Ireland. The detail of such changes is not included in this summary; suffice it to say that:

(a) though the Government of Ireland Act 1920 will be repealed, British legislation will ensure that Northern Ireland remains part of the United Kingdom, and shall not cease to be so without the consent of a majority in the province; in the event of a majority deciding otherwise provision will be made to give effect to their wish;

(b) Articles 2 & 3 of the Constitution of Ireland will be amended (if the Agreement is fully implemented), thus removing the territorial claim to Northern Ireland – by, in effect, shifting the emphasis from 'claim' and 'territory' to 'aspiration' and 'people', and affirming that a united Ireland shall be brought about only by peaceful means and with the consent of a majority of the people, democratically expressed in both jurisdictions in the island.

The Agreement deals with the complex relationships within these islands along three main strands: within Northern Ireland, between North and South in the island of Ireland, and between the islands of Britain and Ireland.

Strand One provides for a democratically elected Assembly in Northern Ireland, which is inclusive in its membership, capable of exercising executive and legislative authority, and subject to safeguards to protect the rights and interests of all sides of the community.

The Assembly, with 108 members elected by Proportional Representation, will exercise full legislative and executive authority on matters currently within the responsibility of Northern Ireland Government Departments, and will be the prime source of authority in respect of all devolved responsibilities.

Safeguards, to ensure that all sections of the community can participate and work together in the Assembly, and that all sections of the community are protected, will include:

the allocation of responsible posts and committee places in proportion to party strengths;

adherence to the European Convention on Human Rights (ECHR) and any Bill of Rights for Northern Ireland supplementing it, and a Human Rights Commission;

arrangements to provide that key decisions and legislation are proofed to ensure that they do not infringe the ECHR or any Bill of Rights for the province;

arrangements to ensure that key decisions are taken on a cross-community basis;

and the establishment of an equality commission.

Detailed arrangements for the operation of the Assembly are set out and include: provision for the Chair and Deputy Chair of the Assembly to be elected on a cross-community basis, with Chairs and Deputy Chairs of Assembly Committees allocated proportionally and membership in broad proportion to party strengths.

Executive Authority will be discharged by a First Minister and

Deputy First Minister (elected on a cross-community basis) and up to 10 Ministers (whose departmental posts will be allocated to parties on the basis of the d'Hondt system [see p. 179] with reference to the number of seats each party has in the Assembly). They will form an Executive Committee, and their duties are clearly set out.

As a condition of appointment all ministers shall affirm the terms of a Pledge of Office (including a commitment to non-violence and exclusively peaceful and democratic means) and undertake to discharge effectively and in good faith all the responsibilities attaching to their office. Both the Pledge of Office and the Code of Conduct demand the highest standards for Ministers. Provision is made for a Minister to be removed from office for failure to meet his or her responsibilities, with specific mention that 'those who hold office should use only democratic, non-violent means and those who do not should be excluded or removed from office under these provisions'.

The Assembly will have authority to pass legislation for Northern Ireland in devolved areas, subject to various safeguards and other criteria; there will also be mechanisms to ensure co-ordination with the Westminster Parliament and to enable parity to be maintained with United Kingdom legislation.

Transitional arrangements: the Assembly will meet first for the purpose of organisation, without legislative or executive powers, to resolve its standing orders and working practices, and make preparations for the effective functioning of the Assembly, as well as the British-Irish Council and the North/South Ministerial Council (see below). During this transitional period also, shadow Ministers shall affirm their commitment to non-violence and exclusively peaceful and democratic means and their opposition to any use or threat of force by others for any political purpose; to work in good faith to bring the new arrangements into being; and to observe the spirit of the Pledge of Office applying to appointed Ministers.

In addition to an Assembly, a consultative Civic Forum, comprising business, trade union and voluntary sectors, to advise on social, economic and cultural issues, will be established.

Strand Two, under the new British-Irish Agreement (pp. 27-29 of *The Agreement*) and legislation yet to be enacted, provides for the establishment of a North/South Ministerial Council, to bring together those with executive responsibilities in Northern Ireland and the Irish Government, to develop consultation, co-operation and action within the island of Ireland – including co-operation through agreed implementation bodies on an all-island and cross-border basis – on matters of mutual interest within the competence of the Administrations, North and South.

Decisions of the Council will be by agreement, with Northern Ireland to be represented by the First Minister, Deputy First Minister and relevant Ministers, and the Irish Government by the Taoiseach and

relevant Ministers. Participation in the Council will be one of the essential responsibilities attaching to relevant posts in the two Administrations. The format and frequency of the meetings and the basic functions of the Council, are set out.

During the transitional period between the elections to the
Assembly and the transfer of power to it, representatives from North
and South will undertake a work programme with a view to agreeing
areas where co-operation and implementation for mutual benefit will
take place; suggestions for such areas are listed.

Strand Three, under the new British-Irish Agreement, provides for
the establishment of a British-Irish Council to promote the harmonious
and mutually beneficial development of the totality of relationships
among the peoples of these islands. Membership of this British-Irish
Council will comprise representatives of the British and Irish Governments, devolved institutions in Northern Ireland, Scotland and Wales,
and also of the Isle of Man and the Channel Islands. It will operate by
consensus, and possible functions, format and frequency of meetings
are set out.

A British-Irish Intergovernmental Conference will be established,
which will subsume both the Anglo-Irish Intergovernmental Council
and the Intergovernmental Conference set up under the 1985 Anglo-
Irish Agreement. This new British-Irish Intergovernmental Conference
will bring together the two Governments to promote bilateral co-operation at all levels on matters of mutual interest within the competence
of both governments. It will meet as required at Summit level, with
both the Prime Minister and Taoiseach present; otherwise, Governments will be represented by appropriate Ministers. All decisions will
be by agreement. There will be no derogation from the sovereignty of
either Government.

In recognition of the Irish Government's special interest in Northern
Ireland, there will be regular meetings of the Conference concerned
with non-devolved Northern Ireland matters, on which the Irish
Government may put forward views and proposals. The Conference
will facilitate co-operation on security matters and address the areas of
rights, justice, prisons and policing in the province. Relevant executive
members of the Northern Ireland Administration will be involved in
Conference meetings.

Under the heading *Rights, Safeguards and Equality of Opportunity* the
parties affirm their commitment to the mutual respect, the civil rights
and the religious liberties of everyone in the community, and against
the background of communal conflict list a wide range of rights that
they specifically affirm. The British Government will complete the incorporation into Northern Ireland law of the European Convention on
Human Rights (ECHR), and establish by legislation a Northern Ireland
Human Rights Commission. The Irish Government will also take steps

to strengthen the protection of human rights in its jurisdiction; further examine the question of the incorporation of the ECHR; establish a Human Rights Commission with a mandate equivalent to that within Northern Ireland; and ratify the Council of Europe Framework Convention on National Minorities (already ratified by the UK).

The participants believe it is essential to acknowledge and address the suffering of the victims of violence as a necessary element of reconciliation, and look forward to the results of the work of the Northern Ireland Victims Commission. They appreciate that support (both statutory and voluntary) will be required to meet the needs of victims; and recognise the good work being done by many organisations to develop reconciliation and mutual understanding.

Pending the devolution of powers to the Northern Ireland Assembly, the British Government will pursue policies that address outstanding economic, social and cultural issues, such as community development and the advancement of women in public life; the problems of a divided society and social cohesion in urban, rural and border areas; combating unemployment and eliminating the differential in unemployment rates between the two communities; and where appropriate and people desire it, promoting minority languages, in particular the Irish language.

Decommissioning of weapons is dealt with under a separate major heading, though in general rather than specific terms. Because of the emotive and sensitive nature of the issue to both traditions in the province, these are set out in full below:

'(i) Participants recall their agreement in the Procedural Motion adopted on 24 September 1997 [see p. 40] "that the resolution of the decommissioning issue is an indispensable part of the process of negotiation", and also recall the provisions of paragraph 25 of Strand I above. [This paragraph refers to the Pledge of Office for Ministers in the Executive of the Assembly.]

(ii) They note the progress made by the Independent International Commission on Decommissioning and the Governments in developing schemes which can represent a workable basis for achieving the decommissioning of illegally-held arms in the possession of paramilitary groups.

(iii) All participants accordingly reaffirm their commitment to the total disarmament of all paramilitary organisations. They also confirm their intention to continue to work constructively and in good faith with the Independent Commission, and to use any influence they may have, to achieve the decommissioning of all paramilitary arms within two years following endorsement in referendums North and South of the agreement and in the context of the implementation of the overall settlement.

(iv) The Independent Commission will continue to monitor, review and verify progress on decommissioning of illegal arms, and will report to both Governments at regular intervals.

(v) Both Governments will take all necessary steps to facilitate the decommissioning process to include bringing the relevant schemes into force by the end of June.'

On *Security*, the participants note that the development of a peaceful environment on the basis of this agreement can and should mean a normalisation of security arrangements.

The British Government will make progress towards the objective of as early a return as possible to normal security arrangements in Northern Ireland, consistent with the level of threat. The Secretary of State will consult on progress, and the response to any paramilitary activity, with the Irish Government and the political parties.

The Irish Government will initiate a review of the Offences Against the State Act.

Regarding *Policing and Justice*, the participants recognise that policing is a central issue in any society, and that Northern Ireland's history of deep divisions has made it highly emotive with great hurt suffered and sacrifices made by many individuals and their families, including those in the RUC. They believe that the agreement provides the opportunity for a new beginning to policing in the province; that it is essential that the police service is professional, efficient, fair, accountable, and free from partisan political control; and that it operates within a coherent and co-operative criminal justice system that conforms with human rights norms. These are some of the reasons given for the establishment of an independent Commission, which will make recommendations for future policing arrangements in the province. There will also be a parallel review of criminal justice.

Regarding *Prisoners*, both Governments will put in place mechanisms for the early release of prisoners convicted of certain specified offences. Prisoners affiliated to organisations that have not established or are not maintaining a complete or unequivocal ceasefire will not benefit from these arrangements. A review process would provide for the advance of the release dates of qualifying prisoners while allowing account to be taken of the seriousness of the offence, etc. The intention would be that should the circumstances allow it, any qualifying prisoners who remained in custody two years after the commencement of the scheme would be released at that point.

Procedures for *Validation, Implementation and Review* will involve the introduction and support by both Governments of appropriate legislation. For example:

'The two Governments will sign a new British-Irish Agreement replacing the 1985 Anglo-Irish Agreement, embodying understandings on constitutional issues and affirming their solemn commitment to support and, where appropriate, implement the agreement reached by the participants in the negotiations which shall be annexed to the British-Irish Agreement.'

(For further details of the British-Irish Agreement see *The Agreement*, pp. 2, 27-30, under the main heading: *Agreement between the Government of The United Kingdom of Great Britain and Northern Ireland and the Government of Ireland*.)

Each Government will organise a *Referendum* on the same day.

In Northern Ireland it will address the question 'Do you support the agreement reached in the multi-party talks on Northern Ireland and set out in Command Paper 3883 ?'

In the South a Bill will first be introduced (a) to amend Articles 2 & 3 of the Constitution of Ireland, and (b) to amend Article 29 to permit the Government to ratify the new British-Irish Agreement. Following its passage the Bill will be put to referendum.

If majorities of those voting in each of the referendums support the Agreement, the Governments will then introduce and support legislation to give effect to all aspects of this agreement, including elections to the Assembly (meeting initially in its 'shadow' mode).

'The establishment of the North/South Ministerial Council, implementation bodies, the British-Irish Council and the British-Irish Intergovernmental Conference, and the assumption by the Assembly of its legislative and executive powers, will take place at the same time on the entry into force of the British-Irish Agreement.'

Arrangements are in place for aspects of the implementation of the multi-party agreement, or the implementation of the agreement as a whole, to be reviewed.

Following implementation, each institution may review any problems that arise in its operation, and take remedial action in consultation with the relevant Government(s). Joint review may also be undertaken with another institution if required. Those difficulties which require amendment of the British-Irish Agreement will fall to the two Governments in consultation with the parties in the Assembly. Each institution will publish an annual report of its operations. The two Governments and the parties in the Assembly will also convene a conference four years after the Agreement comes into effect, to review and report on its operation.

* * *

The d'Hondt System, or 'highest average' method, is named after a Belgian lawyer of the nineteenth century. Seats in the Executive are allocated singly and successively. The 'highest average' secures a seat in the Executive. The method requires the number of seats each party has in the Assembly, to be divided by one, two, three, four, etc, to calculate a 'highest average' when determining each Executive seat. The party divisor is increased by one each time it wins an Executive seat, but not if it does not win such a seat. Each time the divisor changes it is still used against the number of Assembly seats the party holds.

(After the explanation published in the *Belfast Telegraph*, 15 April, 1998.)

APPENDIX II

Quotation from the Letter sent by the Prime Minister to David Trimble
immediately prior to the acceptance of the Good Friday Agreement
– 10 April 1998.

'I understand your problem with paragraph 25 of Strand I is that it requires decisions on those who should be excluded or removed from office in the Northern Ireland Executive to be taken on a cross-community basis.

This letter is to let you know that if, during the course of the first six months of the shadow Assembly or the Assembly itself, these provisions have been shown to be ineffective, we will support changes to these provisions to enable them to be made properly effective in preventing such people from holding office.

Furthermore, I confirm that in our view the effect of the decommissioning section of the agreement, with decommissioning schemes coming into effect in June, is that the process of decommissioning should begin straight away.'

(As reprinted in the *News Letter*, 29 March 1999)

APPENDIX III

Quotation from a Speech of the Prime Minister, Tony Blair
– Belfast, 14 May, 1998

'In clarifying whether the terms and spirit of the agreement are being met and whether violence has genuinely been given up for good there are a range of factors to take into account:

First and foremost, a clear and unequivocal commitment that there is an end to violence for good on the part of republicans and loyalists alike, and that the so-called war is finished, done with, gone; that as the agreement says, non-violence and exclusively peaceful and democratic means are the only means to be used;

That again, as the agreement expressly states, the ceasefires are indeed complete and unequivocal: an end to bombings, killings and beatings, claimed or unclaimed, an end to targeting and procurement of weapons, progressive abandonment and dismantling of paramilitary structures actively directing and promoting violence;

Full co-operation with the Independent Commission on decommissioning to implement the provisions of the agreement; and no other organisations being deliberately used as proxies for violence.'

(From the full distributed version of the text as published in *The Irish News*)

APPENDIX IV
Text of 'Pledge' given by the Prime Minister – Coleraine, 20 May 1998

'My pledge to the people of Northern Ireland:

No change in the status of Northern Ireland without the express consent of the people of Northern Ireland;

Power to take decisions returned to a Northern Ireland Assembly with accountable north-south co-operation;

Fairness and equality guaranteed for all;

Those who use or threaten violence excluded from the government of Northern Ireland;

Prisoners kept in unless violence ended for good.

Whatever the referendum result, as Prime Minister of the United Kingdom, I will continue to work for stability and prosperity for all the people of Northern Ireland.

Tony Blair'

(Displayed in large hand-written and signed poster form as a backdrop to his speech at the University of Ulster)

APPENDIX V
Text of the Declaration agreed at Hillsborough Castle between the British and Irish Governments, 1 April 1999.

'It is now one year since the Good Friday agreement was concluded. Last May it was emphatically endorsed by the people, north and south, and as such it now represents their democratic will.

The agreement, in its own words, offers a truly historic opportunity for a new beginning. It gives us a chance, in this generation, to transcend the bitter legacy of the past and to transform relationships within Northern Ireland, between north and south, and between these islands.

All parties firmly believe that the violence we have all lived through must be put behind us.

Never again should we or our children have to suffer the consequences of conflict. It must be brought to a permanent end. In partnership together we want to ensure a future free from conflict.

The realisation of that future places a heavy obligation on us all, individually and collectively.

The implementation in full of the Agreement is inevitably a lengthy and complex process, involving continuing effort and commitment on all our parts.

It is encouraging and important that, even though much remains to be done, very substantial progress has already been made in turning the promise of the Agreement into a reality.

We must not forget or underplay how far we have come.

Balanced changes to both the Irish constitution and to British consti-

tutional legislation based on the principle of consent, have been approved and are now ready to take effect.

The Northern Ireland Assembly was elected last June and has been
preparing for devolution.

The international agreements signed in Dublin on March 8 provide
for the establishment of the North-South Ministerial Council and
Implementation Bodies, the British-Irish Council and the British-Irish
Intergovernmental Conference.

The Northern Ireland Human Rights Commission has been established and its members appointed, and the new Equality Commission
has been legislated for. Comparable steps by the Irish government are
well under way.

The needs of victims of violence, and their families, including those
of the disappeared, are being addressed in both jurisdictions, though
we acknowledge that for many their pain and suffering will never end.

The commitments in the Agreement in relation to economic, social
and cultural issues, including as regards the Irish language, are being
carried forward, though much of this work is inevitably long term.

Steps have been taken towards normalisation of security arrangements and practices, while the Commission on Policing for Northern
Ireland and the review of criminal justice are both well advanced in
their vital work.

Numerous prisoners, in both jurisdictions, have benefited from
mechanisms providing for their accelerated release.

Against this background there is agreement among all parties that
decommissioning is not a precondition but is an obligation deriving
from their commitment in the agreement, and that it should take place
within the timescale envisaged in the agreement, and through the efforts of the Independent International Commission on Decommissioning.

Sinn Féin have acknowledged these obligations but are unable to indicate the timescale on which decommissioning will begin. They do not
regard the agreement as imposing any requirement to make a start before the establishment of the new institutions. The UUP do not wish to
move to the establishment of the new institutions without some evident
progress with decommissioning.

It would be a tragedy if this difference of view about timing and the
sequence of events prevented the implementation of the agreement
from advancing.

We believe that decommissioning will only happen against a background where implementation is actively moving forward. Continued
progress in establishing the new institutions will in itself create confidence. On the other hand, it is understandable that those who take the
next steps in implementation should seek to be assured that these steps
are not irrevocable if, in the event, no progress is made with decommissioning.

We therefore propose the following way forward:

On (date to be set) nominations will be made under the d'Hondt procedure [p. 179] of those to take up office as ministers when powers are devolved.

At a date to be proposed by the Independent International Commission on Decommissioning but not later than (one month after nomination date) a collective act of reconciliation will take place.

This will see some arms put beyond use on a voluntary basis, in a manner which will be verified by the Independent International Commission on Decommissioning, and further moves on normalisation and demilitarisation in recognition of the improved situation on security.

In addition to the arrangements in respect of military materials, there will at the time be ceremonies of remembrance of all victims of violence, to which representatives of all parties and the two governments, and all churches, will be invited.

Around the time of the act of reconciliation, powers will be devolved and the British-Irish agreement will enter into force.

The following institutions will then be established:

the North-South Ministerial Council,

the North-South Implementation Bodies,

the British-Irish Council

and the British-Irish Intergovernmental Conference.

By (one month after nomination date) the Independent International Commission on Decommissioning will make a report on progress. It is understood by all that the successful implementation of the agreement will be achieved if these steps are taken within the proposed timescales; if they are not taken, the nominations mentioned above will fall to be confirmed by the assembly.'

(As published by *The Irish News*, 2 April 1999)

APPENDIX VI

The Way Forward: A joint statement by the British and Irish governments
– 2 July 1999

'After five days of discussion, the British and Irish governments have put to all the parties a way forward to establish an inclusive Executive, and to decommission arms.

These discussions have been difficult. But as they conclude, the peace process is very much alive, and on track.

The Good Friday Agreement presents the best chance of peace and prosperity in decades. It is clear from our discussions that nobody wants to throw that opportunity away.

We believe that unionist and nationalist opinion will see that our approach meets their concerns, and will support it accordingly.

The way forward is as follows:

1. All parties reaffirm the three principles agreed on 25 June:
an inclusive executive exercising devolved powers;
decommissioning of all paramilitary arms by May 2000;
decommissioning to be carried out in a manner determined by the
International Commission on Decommissioning.

2. The D'Hondt procedure to nominate ministers to be run on July 15. [See p. 179]

3. The Devolution Order to be laid before the British parliament on July 16 to take effect on July 18. Within the period specified by the de Chastelain Commission, the Commission will confirm the start to the process of decommissioning, that start to be defined as in their report of July 2.

4. As described in their report of yesterday, the Commission will have urgent discussions with the groups' points of contact. The Commission will specify that actual decommissioning is to start within a specified time. They will report progress in September and December 1999 and in May 2000.

5. A 'failsafe' clause: the governments undertake that, in accordance with the review provisions of the Agreement, if commitments under the Agreement are not met, either in relation to decommissioning or to devolution, they will automatically, and with immediate effect, suspend the operations of the institutions set up by the Agreement. In relation to decommissioning, this action will be taken on receipt of a report at any time that the commitments now being entered into or steps which are subsequently laid down by the Commission, are not fulfilled, in accordance with the Good Friday Agreement. The British Government will legislate to this effect.

All parties have fought very hard to ensure their basic concerns have been met. This means we are now closer than ever to fulfilling the promise of the Good Friday Agreement:

a government for Northern Ireland in which the two traditions work together in a devolved administration;

new North-South and British-Irish institutions;

the decommissioning of paramilitary arms;

constitutional change;

equality, justice, human rights, and the normalisation of Northern Ireland society.

All sides have legislative safeguards to ensure that commitments entered into are met.

This is an historic opportunity. Now is the time to seize it.'

(As published by the *Newsletter* and the *Belfast Telegraph, 3 July 1999*.)

The De Chastelain Report, 11 February, 2000

1. In our report of 31 January 2000, the commission reported that the intense negotiations were continuing and that we would report any concrete result that came from them. Since then we have had several contacts with the IRA and loyalist representatives.

2. The IRA declaration of support for the peace process leading to a permanent peace in Ireland, the contribution made by the ceasefires and the statement that the IRA provides no threat to that process are recognised.

We believe that these are important issues of considerable significance for peace and stability in Northern Ireland and they were reflected in our 31 January report.

3. Since December 1999, the IRA has engaged frankly and helpfully with the commission and we note their intention to continue to do so.

4. We also note the IRA assessment that the question of British forces and loyalist paramilitaries in Northern Ireland must be addressed. While the future of British troops is outside our remit, the elimination of the threat posed by the loyalist paramilitary arms is clearly within the commission's remit.

We have been advised by loyalist representatives of their commitment to address the issue of arms in the context of similar action taken by the IRA.

In our discussions this week with the UVF and UFF representatives, each confirmed their positions as stated in our 31 January report and the UFF representatives further engaged with us on methods of decommissioning and related support issues.

5. We welcome the IRA's belief that the 'state of perpetual crisis' can be averted and that the issue of arms can be resolved.

We find particularly significant and view as valuable progress the assertion made to us by the IRA respresentative that the IRA will consider how to put arms and explosives beyond use, in the context of the full implementation of the Good Friday Agreement, and in the context of the removal of the causes of conflict.

6. The commission welcomes the IRA's recognition that the issue of arms needs to be dealt with in an acceptable way and that this is a necessary objective of a genuine peace process and their statement that for those reasons they are engaged with us.

The commission further welcomes the IRA's commitment to sustain and enhance its contribution to a durable peace and their statement that they have supported and will continue to support efforts to secure the resolution of the arms issue.

7. The representative indicated to us today the context in which the IRA will initiate a comprehensive process to put arms beyond use, in a man-

ner as to ensure maximum public confidence.

8. The commission believes that this commitment, on the basis described above, holds out the real prospect of an agreement which would enable it to fulfil the substance of its mandate. We will make a further report to the two governments as appropriate.

(The report is signed by Tauno Nieminen, John de Chastelain and Andrew D. Sens. As published in The Irish Times, 12 February, 2000)

Bibliography

Adamson, I., *The Ulster People*, Pretani Press, Bangor, 1991.

Bannerman, J., 'The Scots of Dalriada', in *Who are the Scots?*, edited G. Menzies, B.B.C., London, 1971.

Bardon, J., *A History of Ulster*, The Blackstaff Press, Belfast, 1992.

Beckett, J. C., (a) *The Making of Modern Ireland*, Faber & Faber, London and Boston, 1966.

Beckett, J. C., (b) *The Anglo-Irish Tradition*, The Blackstaff Press, Belfast, 1976.

Bew, P. & Gillespie, G., (a) *Northern Ireland – A Chronology of the Troubles 1968-1993*, Gill & Macmillan, Dublin, 1993.

Bew, P. & Gillespie, G., (b) *The Northern Ireland Peace Process 1993-1996 – A Chronology*, Serif, London, 1996.

Byrne, F. J., (a) *Irish Kings and High-Kings*, B.T.Batsford Ltd., London, 1973.

Byrne, F.J., (b) 'Early Irish Society', in *The Course of Irish History*, edited T. W. Moody & F. X. Martin, R.T.E. and Mercier Press, Cork, 1967.

Catherwood, C., *Crash Course on Church History*, Hodder & Stoughton, London, 1998.

Chadwick, N., *The Celts*, Pelican Books, 1971, reprinted Penguin Books, Harmondsworth, Mddx., 1987.

Chalmers, G., *Caledonia*, London, 1807, new edition, Alexander Gardner, Paisley, 1887.

Churchill, W. S., *A History of the English-speaking Peoples*, Cassell & Company Ltd., London, 1956, first cheap edition 1962.

Cosgrove,A., 'The Gaelic Resurgence and the Geraldine Supremacy', in *The Course of Irish History*, edited T. W. Moody & F. X. Martin, R.T.E. and Mercier Press, Cork, 1967.

Cromie, H., *Ulster Settlers in America*, Presbyterian Church in Ireland, Belfast, 1976.

Curtis, E., *A History of Ireland*, Methuen & Co. Ltd., London, 1936,

Dunlop, J., *A Precarious Belonging – Presbyterians and the Conflict in Ireland*, The Blackstaff Press, Belfast, 1995.

Edwards, R. D., (a) *The Faithful Tribe – An Intimate Portrait of the Loyal Institutions*, Harper Collins, London,1999.

Edwards, R.D., (b) 'Sons of Ulster striding headlong into the abyss', *Sunday Independent*, Dublin, August 4 1996.

Fitzpatrick, R., *God's Frontiersmen – The Scots-Irish Epic*, Weidenfield & Nicolson, London, 1989.

Foster, R.F., *Modern Ireland 1600-1972*, Penguin Books, Harmondsworth, Mddx.,1989.

Fowler, J. T., *Adamnani – Vita S. Columbae, edited from Dr. Reeves' Text with Introduction and Notes*, Oxford, 1894.

Gregory, A., *Cuchulain of Muirthemne*, 5th Edn., Colin Smythe, Gerrards Cross, 1970.

Hanna, C. A., *The Scotch-Irish*, G. P. Putman's Sons, New York & London,1902, reprinted The Genealogical Publishing Co., Baltimore, 1968.

Hanna, R., *Land of the Free – Ulster and the American Revolution*, Ulster Society (Publications) Limited, Lurgan, 1992.

Hanna, W. A., *Celtic Migrations*, Pretani Press, Belfast, 1985.

Harris, M., *The Catholic Church and the Formation of the Northern Irish State*, Cork University Press, Cork, 1994.

Hayes-McCoy, G. A., 'The Tudor Conquest', in *The Course of Irish History*, edited T. W. Moody & F. X. Martin, R.T.E. and Mercier Press, Cork, 1967.

Henderson, I., 'The Problem of the Picts', in *Who are the Scots?* edited G. Menzies, B.B.C., London,1971.

Hill, G., *An Historical Account of the MacDonnells of Antrim*, Archer & Sons, Belfast, 1873.

Holmes, R. F. G., (a) *Our Irish Presbyterian Heritage*, Publications Committee, Presbyterian Church in Ireland, Belfast, 1985.

Holmes, R. F. G., (b) *The Presbyterian Church in Ireland: A Popular History*, The Columba Press, Dublin, 1999.

Kearney, H., *The British Isles – A History of Four Nations*, Cambridge University Press, 1989.

Kennedy, Billy, (a) *The Scots-Irish in the Hills of Tennessee*, Causeway Press, Londonderry, 1995.

Kennedy, Billy, (b) *The Scots-Irish in the Shenandoah Valley*, Causeway Press, Londonderry, 1996.

Kennedy, Billy, (c) *The Scots-Irish in the Carolinas*, Causeway Press, Londonderry, 1997.

Kinsella, T., *The Tain*, Oxford University Press, London, 1970, reprinted 1979.

Kinahan, T., (a) *Where do we go from here? – Protestants and the Future of Northern Ireland*, The Columba Press, Dublin, 1995.

Kinahan, T., (b) *A More Excellent Way – A Vision for Northern Ireland*, The Corrymeela Press, Belfast, 1998.

Leyburn, J. G., *The Scotch-Irish*, The University of North Carolina Press, Chapel Hill, 1962.

McBride, I., *Scripture Politics – Ulster Presbyterians and Irish Radicalism in the late Eighteenth Century*, (Appendix – 'Presbyterian Ministers and Probationers Suspected of Involvement in the 1798 Rebellion'), Oxford University Press, Oxford, 1998.

McKerlie, P. H., *Galloway in Ancient and Modern Times*, W. Blackwood & Sons, Edinburgh, 1891.

McMillan, W., 'Presbyterian Ministers and the Ulster Rising' in *Protestant, Catholic and Dissenter: The Clergy in 1798*, edited L. Swords, The Columba Press, Dublin, 1997.

MacNeill, E., 'The Pretannic Background in Britain and Ireland', *Journal of the Royal Society of Antiquaries of Ireland*, LXIII, 1-28, 1933.

MacNiocaill, G., *Ireland before the Vikings*, Gill & Macmillan Ltd., Dublin, 1972, reprinted 1980.

MacQueen, J., 'Welsh and Gaelic in Galloway', in *Transactions and Journal of the Proceedings of the Dumfriesshire and Galloway Natural History and Antiquarian Society*, XXXII, 77-92, 1953.

Meyers, K., 'Oranges without bitterness', *The Daily Telegraph*, London, June 20, 1999.

Moss, Bobby G., 'Scots-Irish Loyalists in the American Revolution', in *The Scots-Irish in the Carolinas*, by Billy Kennedy, The Causeway Press, Londonderry, 1997.

Nicolaisen, W. F. H., *Scottish Place-Names*, B. T. Batsford Ltd., London, 1976, paperback edition, 1989.

Ó Corráin, D., *Ireland before the Normans*, Gill & Macmillan Ltd., Dublin, 1972, reprinted 1980.

Ó Fiaich, T., 'The Celts', in *The People of Ireland*, edited P. Loughrey, B.B.C. Northern Ireland and The Appletree Press Ltd., Belfast, 1988.

O'Rahilly, T. F., *Early Irish History and Mythology*, Dublin Institute for Advanced Studies, Dublin, 1946, reprinted 1984.

Owen, T. R., *The Geological Evolution of the British Isles*, Pergamon Press, Oxford, 1976.

Reeves, W., *The Life of St Columba, written by Adamnan, with notes and dissertations*, Irish Archaelogical & Celtic Society, Dublin,1857.

Stewart, A. T. Q., *The Narrow Ground – Aspects of Ulster, 1609-1969*, Faber & Faber, London, 1977.

Thomas, A. C., *Britain and Ireland in Early Christian Times*, Thames & Hudson Ltd., London, 1971.

References

References are to books listed in the bibliography.

1.   Owen, T. R., 14-41.
2.   Byrne, F.J., (a) 69, 107, 113; MacNiocaill, G., 11-13.
3.   Kinsella, T., Translator's Note vii, 6-20, 25-39, 238-253, 257;
   Gregory, A., 35-52, 63-76, 92-117, 141-204.
4.   Henderson, I., 65.
5.   MacNeill, E., 1-28.
6.   Ó Fiaich, T., 27.
7.   Fowler, J. T., Introduction LXX.
8.   Hanna, W. A., 31-32, 35.
9.   Chalmers, G., I. 358-359.
10.   McKerlie, P. H., 9-21, 44-45, 62.
11.   Thomas, A. C., -57.
12.   Nicolaisen,W.F.H., 39-46.
13.   McQueen, J., 77-92.
14.   Bannerman, J., 66-67; Chalmers, G., Genealogical Table p. 278;
   Reeves, W., Genealogical Table to face p. 438.
15.   Chadwick, N., 94.
16.   O'Rahilly, T. F., 81-82; Byrne, F.J., (a) 10, 106-108, 127-129.
17.   O'Rahilly, T. F., 6, 7, 15-17, 80-84, 100.
18.   Byrne, F. J., (a) 10; MacNiocaill, G., 163.
19.   Byrne, F. J., (a) 9, 11, 114; Ó Corráin, D., 76.
20.   Bannerman, J., 66.
21.   Byrne, F. J., (b) 44.
22.   O'Rahilly, T. F., 15-17, 194-197.
23.   Byrne, F. J., (a) 9, 45.
24.   MacNiocaill, G., 14, Map p. 38, 73-78, 89, 96-97.
25.   Fowler, J. T., Genealogical Table to follow p. XCIV; Reeves, W.,
   Genealogical Table to face pp. 342, 438; Chalmers, G.,
   Genealogical Table p.278.
26.   Bannerman, J., 68, 79.
27.   Curtis, E., 83-84.
28.   Bardon, J., 40-41.
29.   Cosgrove, A., 160.
30.   Curtis, E., 94-101.
31.   Cosgrove, A., 158-165; Curtis, E., 131,134-135.

32. Churchill, W. S., I. 388-389, II. 15-17.
33. Hayes-McCoy, G. A., 174.
34. Hill, G., 21-34.
35. Bardon, J., 122; Holmes, R. F. G., (a) 5.
36. Byrne, F. J., 114, 127-129.
37. Curtis, E., 118,181,184-186.
38. Bardon, J., 78-81.
39. Curtis, E., 205-214.
40. Bardon, J., 10-114.
41. Curtis, E., 209-220.
42. Bardon, J., 120-121.
43. Holmes, R. F. G., (a) 4-6.
44. Curtis, E., 226-232.
45. Ibid., 176-177, 199-200.
46. Stewart, A. T. Q., 37-41.
47. Adamson, I., 60.
48. Holmes, R. F. G., (a) 16-19.
49. Ibid., 25.
50. Adamson, I., 63-64.
51. Bardon, J., 135-139; Stewart, A. T. Q., 48-52.
52. Holmes, R. F. G., (a) 27.
53. Becket, J. C., (a) 82-103.
54. Holmes, R. F. G., (a) 35.
55. Curtis, E., 249-255.
56. Holmes, R. F. G., (a) 37; Hanna, C. A., I. 604.
57. Holmes, R. F. G., (a) 44.
58. Adamson, I., 66-67.
59. Churchill, W. S., II. 304-325.
60. Becket, J. C., (a) 139-141.
61. Kearney, H., 128.
62. Churchill, W. S., II. 309, 321- 322, III. 3-5.
63. Foster, R. F., 142.
64. Bardon, J., 152, 155, 157-158.
65. Ibid., 159-164.
66. Becket, J. C., (a) 146-149; Bardon, J., 164-166.
67. Bardon, J., 171.
68. Kearney, H., 128.
69. Bardon, J., 172.
70. Curtis, E., 287-288.
71. Leyburn, J. G., 168-175.
72. Holmes, R. F. G., (a) 80-83.
73. Bardon, J., 220-226.
74. Ibid., 230-231.
75. Beckett, J. C., (a) 262-265.
76. Holmes, R. F. G., (a) 85-90; McBride, I., 81-117; McMillan, W., 232-236; Stewart, A. T. Q., 101-110.

77. Beckett, J. C., (a) 329-331.
78. Bardon, J., 369-370.
79. Beckett, J. C., (a) 364-369.
80. Foster, R. F., 359, 400-405, 415-424.
81. Bardon, J., 415, 431-432, 437-439.
82. Beckett, J. C., (a) 430-434, 440-441, 446-448.
83. Foster, R. F., 516, 518, 534.
84. Beckett, J. C., (b) 151-152.
85. Dunlop, J., 50-54.
86. Harris, M., 256-265.
87. Dunlop, J., 66.
88. Leyburn, J. G., 327-333.
89. Ibid., 157-185.
90. Ibid., 245-246.
91. Moss, Bobby G., 153-158; Leyburn, J. G., 11, 215, 235-236, 253.
92. Leyburn, J. G., 169-175,189, 196, 201, 206, 209-210, 213, 219, 232.
93. Ibid., 191-192.
94. Ibid., 192, 213, 223-236.
95. Fitzpatrick, R., 86, 93.
96. Fitzpatrick, R., 99, 102; Leyburn, J. G., 301-304, 306-307.
97. Fitzpatrick, R., 88-89, 96.
98. Hanna, R., 68; Cromie, H., 49.
99. Leyburn, J. G., 305, 308; Cromie, H., 51-55.
100. Hanna, R., 78, 90, 94; Fitzpatrick, R., 104-105.
101. Leyburn, L. G., 232-235, 274-275, 282-285.
102. Ibid., 331-333.
103. Fitzpatrick, R., 166-168.
104. Leyburn, L. G., 331.
105. Kennedy, Billy, (a) 99-110.
106. Fitzpatrick, R., 136-136; Kennedy, Billy, (b) 111-118.
107. Cromie, H., 62-63.
108. Kennedy, Billy, (c) 46-48.
109. Catherwood, C., 140, 165-168.
110. Dunlop, J., 83-84,86.
111. Bew, P. and Gillespie, G., 63.
112. Myers, K., 13.